JOHN C. DVORAK'S

PC CRASH COURSE
AND SURVIVAL GUIDE

WITH PETER HARRISON & STEVEN FRANKEL

We wish to thank:

Studio Etyd AB, Inglestad, Sweden; design and artwork

Scandinavian PC Systems, Inc.
51 Monroe Street, Suite 1101,
Rockville, Maryland 20850 USA
1-800-288-SCAN or 1-301-294-7450 (sales)
1-301-294-7453 (information or help)
1-301-251-1053 (fax)

Scandinavian PC Systems (UK) Ltd.
36 Hawkes Drive
Heathcote Industrial Estate
Warwick CV34 6LX
United Kingdom
+ 44 926336695 (fax)
+ 44 926314334

Scandinavian PC Systems
P.O. Box 5004 S-350 05 Växjö
Sweden + 46 47015400
          + 46 47023537 (fax)

First Printing December, 1989
Second Printing February, 1990
Third Printing March, 1990
Fourth Printing June, 1990

ISBN #91-878322-05-2

Library of Congress Catalog Card Number: 89-92722

Foreword

By John C. Dvorak

If the desktop computer revolution is missing anything, it's this book. For some reason, unknown to me or any other person who writes for this industry, there has been a paucity of good entry-level books which introduce newcomers and amateurs to the world of the PC. This is particularly alarming since the PC requires some effort to master. A kid can do it, sure, but not without some help. Because there are no helpful books for beginners, we have developed some peculiar users. My favorite was outlined in a 1989 *PC Magazine* column I wrote. I described them as the "dead-end" users. These are people who use one or two programs on their PC and are fearful to even try anything new. They are unfamiliar with the basic operation of a computer and shaky when it comes to the simple DOS commands which are available. I can't begin to imagine how many PC users cannot even format a diskette. It's pathetic.

One of my most popular columns over the years has been a series I wrote about some of the bonehead things new PC users have done, such as taking a disk out of the sleeve or folding a 5 1/4-inch disk so it could be shoved into a 3 1/2-inch drive. When I asked the readers for real life anecdotes I was swamped with stories.

But can we blame the users for these idiocies when the hapless user can't even find a beginners' book on using a PC? Does a person have to find a college class just to boot DOS?

In the early days of the microcomputer revolution things were different. An entire generation was raised on numerous beginners' books and a slew of magazines which were mostly in the mood to tell us all about the new technology – to teach us. The magazines could get away with this approach for only a year or two. As the base of readers learned the basics of computing, the magazines had to either raise the level of expertise to that of the now knowledgeable reader or risk losing the readers. Since magazines, like any business, prefer the old customer (the renewal) to the new customer and constant turbulent turnover, the magazines slowed down their educational process and slowly evolved to the news and reviews magazines that are so popular today. Todays' magazine is written for the knowledgeable computer user who already knows a lot and wants to know more and more.

If a hapless beginner stumbles into the pages of the better magazines and starts to read about DOS shells and command processors and 33 megahertz chips, he or she is soon a nervous wreck wondering what all this talk means. So if you weren't around the computer scene in 1976 so you could learn the basics from all the sources talking basics, then you were out of luck. During this period the books also reflected the scene and numerous books (like the one you're now reading) were on computer store book racks. These books excited people. They resulted in computer sales. Nowadays the stores send people in the field to drum up corporate accounts and to heck with the newcomer. By 1980, the books for beginners disappeared and a new priesthood of experts began to emerge. They gave seminars, told people what to buy, pontificated. All the while the newcomer was shunned.

I joined this project with Peter Harrison and the fellows at Scandinavian PC Systems to help produce this latest edition of this book because I think it's sorely needed. It's a book that is an easy reference and a perfect companion for anyone who wants to learn about his PC. It's a book for newcomers who wonder what to buy and it's a terrific reference for the new computer owner who wants to learn how the machine works and how to get the most out of it.

Preface

Welcome to **PC Press/Scandinavian PC Systems'** world of inexpensive, simple, and efficient computer books and programs. This book is designed to teach you **the least amount of detail you need to know** to use an IBM-PC-type personal computer. The programs supplied with this book allow you to test your knowledge of what you've learned.

About This Book

This book is divided into eleven chapters, and contains five useful appendices. If you are eager to try out the programs supplied with this book, the necessary information is given in the appendices. You will, however, need to know how to format a diskette before you can proceed with these programs. If you are uncertain as to what formatting is, then you should try to hold back your enthusiasm and read the first few chapters before using the programs.

Also, even if you don't already own a computer, you can derive a lot of benefit by reading this book. Reading it is an excellent way to prepare yourself for talking to computer salespersons, or the "techies" in your office. After going through it you'll know all the basics needed to converse with them intelligently.

The following topics are covered in this book:

1. *PC – What's That?*
   Gives you some general information about computers by introducing the parts and providing some basic ideas of what a computer can really do.

2. *Starting Your Computer*
   Tells you how to start your computer. Also tells you what the strange messages that you get actually mean.

3. *Some Important Beginnings*
   Teaches you how to prepare diskettes for use and check their contents. Step-by-step exercises are included.

4. *Copying and Deleting Files*
   Shows you how to copy information between diskettes and delete information from them. Step-by-step exercises are included.

5. *One Step Further*
Now it's time to learn about a few more commands and concepts, including ones with strange names such as wild cards and screen dumping. Naturally, step-by-step exercises are included.

6. *The Secrets of a Hard Disk*
Introduces you to both the complexities and benefits of a hard disk. You'll learn the basic commands and the theory that's needed to organize and use them effectively. This chapter is written so that even readers who don't have a hard disk yet can understand it. Need we say that step-by-step exercises are included?

7. *How to Sound Like a Techie, Even If You Aren't One*
This chapter explains a lot of the computer jargon that's thrown around. It's an easy-to-understand technical chapter for non-technically minded people.

8. *Communications Crash Course*
Teaches you the least you need to know to come to terms with the complicated world of computer communications.

9. *Living With a Computer*
Discusses setting up a computer workspace in today's market and how to protect your investment.

10. *The Smart Buyer's Guide to Acquiring Hardware and Software*
Tells you what you need to know to intelligently purchase hardware and software.

11. *An OS/2 Briefing*
Contains brief reflections on the arrival of OS/2, and its importance.

The appendices cover the following topics:

Appendix A. Using the Optional Diskette

Appendix B. Some Useful DOS Commands

Appendix C. Some Common DOS Error Messages

Appendix D. The Keys On Your Keyboard

Appendix E. Producing Graphics Characters with the **Alt** Key

Different Typefaces Used

To make it easier for you to read and understand this manual, we have used different typefaces as follows:

- Items that you are to type on the keyboard are printed in color and in a different typeface:

  ```
  do this
  ```

- Items that appear on the screen are printed in a different typeface, and are boxed in, as shown below:

```
Screen display
```

- Items which refer to something displayed on your screen are shown as follows:

  ```
  This refers to something shown on your screen.
  ```

- Whenever we refer to specific keys, we print either the symbol, or the keyname as follows:

  ↵

  or

  Home

You should be aware that screen displays shown in this book are only examples, and frequently will differ from those that are displayed on your screen. This isn't our fault or – more importantly – yours. There are literally thousands of different combinations of computer parts and operating systems that all are considered part of the IBM-PC family of computers and clones, and each does things just a little bit differently.

How to Contact PC Press/ Scandinavian PC Systems

If you need help or information about other products, you may contact PC Press/Scandinavian PC Systems in the following ways:

By Mail:

PC Press/Scandinavian PC Systems Inc.
51 Monroe Street, Suite 1101
Rockville, MD 20850

By Phone:

1-800-288-SCAN or 301-294-7450 (sales)
1-301-294-7453 (information or help)

By Fax:

1-301-251-1053

PLEASE KEEP IN TOUCH!

Table of Contents

PC – What's That?

Chapter 1   The initials PC stand for *Personal Computer*, the collective name given to a whole range of computers. This chapter introduces you to personal computers, and assumes that you have no prior knowledge of them.

A Little History

The first electronic computer was produced as long ago as 1946. It was called ENIAC, and comprised more than 18,000 vacuum tubes, the kind used in old-fashioned radio and television sets. As you can imagine it was a very large machine, occupying most of a whole building. It weighed 30 tons, which is about as much as 30 small cars. ENIAC was in use for about 10 years, but despite its colossal size it could not do more than today's simple pocket calculators.

In 1975, the first home computers were launched. Among the first producers were such familiar companies as Apple, Commodore, and Tandy. Atari launched its first computer aimed at both home users and small companies in 1979, and about a year later the first small business computers, such as the Osborne I and Kaypro II, were launched.

A very significant year for the development of computers was 1981, when IBM launched its first personal computer. Since then, computers have developed at a fast clip. Today's personal computers are faster, have a much larger capacity, and cost only a fraction of a 1981 model.

A personal computer is a complete system which can be placed on your desk. It can perform a whole range of tasks at very high speeds.

Many companies adopted the standards set by the IBM PC to produce their own computers, which work in the same way as the IBM machines. These are often referred to as *IBM compatible* computers, or *IBM clones*. Both the IBM PC and its compatibles have undergone enormous development, with improvements being announced every few months. This has resulted in newer models with names such as the XT, AT, 286, 386, and PS/2. These different models are discussed later on in this chapter.

What Is a Computer, Really?

In simple terms, a computer is no more than an electrical appliance. Like your television, or freezer, it has been developed to be able to perform certain tasks. For example, you can use your computer as a typewriter for writing letters, as a pocket calculator to balance your checkbook, or as a VCR/TV combo to display pictures and drawings. You can also use it to store telephone numbers, play games, produce technical drawings and develop camera-ready documents for printing. Computers can even be used to run production lines. Just like any other electrical appliance, computers can and do break down and cause problems. However, be very skeptical when a mistake is blamed "on the computer." In most cases it's a human error that causes you to receive that notice from the phone company that says that unless you pay your outstanding bill for $4,567,333.13, your telephone will be disconnected.

A computer is not some sort of supernatural, super-intelligent, all-mighty machine poised to take over the world. A computer can not think for itself, it can only follow instructions. It is not capable of suddenly deciding that it would like to have an ice-cream cone, or of feeling the desire to take a long vacation on some sunny island beach. It can however, follow instructions and perform predefined tasks at an amazingly high rate: a million or so instructions per second.

Assume that you have a list of telephone numbers stored in your computer system, and a program, or predefined list of instructions, which can extract the right number for a given person. If you ask your computer what telephone number Abraham Lincoln has, it will probably, after a short delay, tell you that it can not find his number. It is not capable, however, of answering directly that Lincoln was alive 200 years ago and does not, and did not, have a telephone.

If you ask your computer to print out 2+5=9, it will do so. Again, it is not capable of thinking for itself and telling you that 2+5 does not equal 9. It also can't refuse to print lies. On the other hand, by giving the computer the right information it could, for example, calculate the wages for thousands of employees in a large company in a matter of seconds.

By giving a computer an appropriate set of instructions, it can very quickly perform a wide range of tasks. A computer is a very fast working, but completely stupid, machine.

The Different Parts of a Computer

While their appearance varies, the basic parts which make up a personal computer are the same. All computers need some way of allowing the user to give instructions or information (*keyboard*), and some way of showing what's going on (*monitor* or *screen*). Other important parts needed are a place in which information can be stored (*disks* or *hard disks*), and the mechanism that can serve as a traffic cop and control the flow of information within the computer (*system unit*). You also need a means of making your data accessible to people who don't have a computer handy (*printer*).

The Keyboard

The keyboard has a layout that's similar to a typewriter, but it has several extra keys.

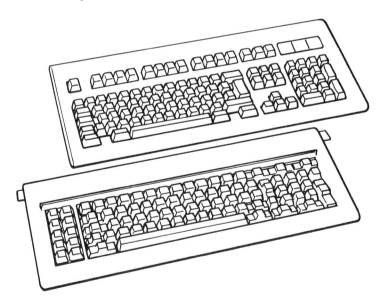

The keyboard is used to send instructions to the computer and to input required information or *data*. Many beginners are slightly wary of pressing keys because they do not understand what happens. They're worried that they can destroy the computer in some way if they press the wrong combination of keys. This is not the case, however.

The different keys on the keyboard are discussed more fully in Appendix *D. The Keys On Your Keyboard*.

The Monitor

The monitor is rather like a television set, although it does not function in quite the same way. Its display is the computer's way of showing you what's going on. It can also be referred to as the *video display terminal* (*VDT*), the *video display unit* (*VDU*), or simply as the *screen*. There is a third term, *cathode ray tube* (*CRT*), which is often used synonymously with VDT and VDU. All of these terms are used to refer to the display unit on a computer.

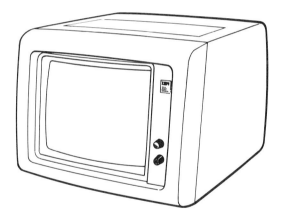

There are many kinds of monitors, but the main difference is between *monochrome* models that can only display images in varying shades of amber, green, or gray, and *color* monitors that can reproduce the full visual spectrum. A color monitor will often brighten up the time you spend working with your computer. On the other hand, a monochrome monitor costs less, is more compact and will often suffice for your needs.

The monitor is used to show information which your computer send out, such as a letter you've typed, the results of a calculation, or even a picture.

The System Unit

The system unit is the central part of a computer. All other units, like the monitor and the keyboard, are connected to and controlled by this unit.

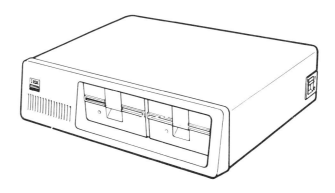

The system unit processes your keyboard inputs and controls the output to your monitor. It also processes all instructions it's given and all relevant data for each task it performs. All calculations are done within the system unit.

The Computer's Memory

An integral part of the system unit is the computer's memory, where text and numbers are stored. For example, a number can be stored in the computer's memory and retrieved later to be used in a multiplication operation.

There are two very different sorts of memory: *ROM* memory and *RAM* memory. These are described below.

ROM Memory

ROM is a permanent memory. Data stored in ROM contains information your computer needs when you first turn it on. ROM stands for *Read Only Memory,* which means that you can never change its contents. Your computer can only read and use the information that is stored there. Information in ROM remains even when your computer is off.

RAM Memory

RAM is a nonpermanent memory and it's there that data is stored temporarily while you are working with the computer. Text and numbers can be saved as long as they are needed for a specific task, but they will disappear from RAM when the computer is turned off or when a different computer program is activated. RAM stands for *Random Access Memory*, which refers to the concept that data can be written to, and read from, this sort of memory at will.

Memory Size

The size of your computer's memory is measured in *bytes*, or *kilobytes*. Each byte is the same as one character. For example, the text, "How nice you are!" would take up 17 bytes, not forgetting the blanks and the exclamation point. A kilobyte is 1024 bytes, and it's sometimes just called *K*, or *Kb*.

The important thing, from the user's point of view, is the size of the computer's RAM-type memory. Programs are loaded into RAM, and larger programs require larger RAM. If your computer's RAM is too small, you will not be able to run some of the larger programs.

Most computers these days have 640K RAM, which is 640 kilobytes, i.e., about 640,000 bytes (or, more exactly, 655,360 bytes). Older computers often have less memory; 256K, or 512K, while newer computers may have 1 or 2 *megs* or *Mb* (million bytes) of RAM. It is possible to increase the size of the memory with add-on circuit boards called *cards* that can plug into your system's unit.

Data Storage

One of the most important aspects of a computer is its capability to store and recall information. When you are creating a document, for example, the text is stored in RAM, but this means that all information disappears when you turn the computer off. You can, however, make a copy of that information on a *floppy disk* or *hard disk*. This allows you, at a later time, to recall the stored information and load it into your computer again. You can then extend, edit, or erase the document.

Floppy Disks

Floppy disks, sometimes referred to as *floppies* or *floppy diskettes*, are small plastic wafers covered with magnetic particles that are used for storing information. There are basically two types of floppy disks, 3.5″ and 5.25″ disks, which refer to the actual diameter of the disks in inches.

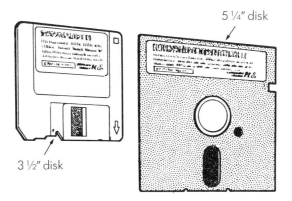

5 ¼″ disk

3 ½″ disk

Each disk can store a certain amount of kilobytes of information, but this does not depend on the physical size of the disk.

- 3.5″ disks can store 360K, 720K, or 1.44 Mb (1440 K)

- 5.25″ disks can store 360K, or 1.2M (usually referred to as *high density disks*).

As an example, a 360K disk can store the equivalent of about 200 pages of printed text.

Floppy disks can be moved between computers, assuming that both computers are IBM compatible and have the same kind of disk drives. You can, for example, create a text on your computer at work, save a copy of that text on a floppy disk, and take it home with you for use on your own computer.

Disk Drives

The use of floppy disks requires a *disk drive*. This is a unit that reads and records information on floppy disks. It's normally mounted in the system unit, although it is possible to have a free-standing unit.

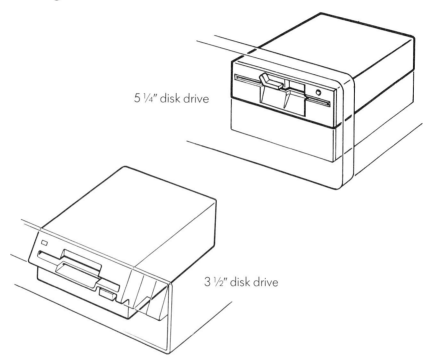

5 ¼″ disk drive

3 ½″ disk drive

All computers have at least one such disk drive, and most have two. Units for 3.5″ floppies are becoming more and more common, and you may see some PCs that sport a 5.25″ disk drive that can read only 360K floppies, a 5.25″ unit that reads 1.2M floppies and a 3.5″ unit that reads 360K, 720K and 1.44M disks. If the owner is a man, it's likely that he goes to work wearing both a belt and suspenders!

To use a floppy disk, you just insert the disk into the available slot. Most 5.25″ units also require you to push a lever down or close a door to enable it to function properly.

Hard Disks

A hard disk is a rigid set of disks that are mounted permanently within the system unit.

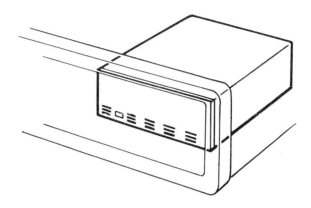

Although it is possible to remove a hard disk drive and install it in another computer, it is very unusual to move hard disks around between computers. Having said this, it is worth mentioning that there are also portable hard disk drives, which use specially designed cases to make it easy to remove and refit them. A hard disk is a set of disks, with multiple *read and write heads* that allow it to store and access very large amounts of data very quickly. A small hard disk can store 20M of data, which is the equivalent of about 10,000 pages of text. Larger hard disks can store anywhere from 30 to 300 megs, and units that can store several *gigabytes* (billion bytes) of data are rapidly becoming affordable.

A computer that has a hard disk is much better equipped than one that doesn't have a hard disk. Many larger programs now require a hard disk; and, since they operate three to ten times faster than a floppy drive, their use is habit forming. Once you use a hard disk for some length of time, you'll never want to use a machine that doesn't have one again.

ABC For Disk Drives

Your computer will automatically give a name to each of the disk drives in your system. The letters A:, B:, C: etc. are used. This is done so that it is possible to keep track of which drive the computer is working with.

- The first floppy disk drive is called drive A:.

Diskette drive A

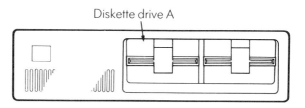

- The second floppy disk drive is called drive B:.

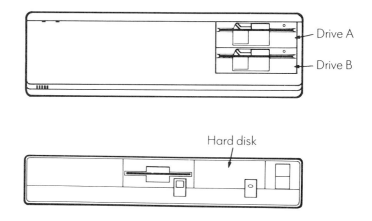

Drive A

Drive B

Hard disk

- The first hard disk drive is called drive **C:**, even if you do not have a floppy disk drive named B:.

- Subsequent disk drives, whether hard or floppy (Remember our belts-and-suspender type user?), are named **D:, E:, F:,** etc.

Printers

Although a printer is not actually part of a computer, it's the most common addition to one. You would not create letters and other documents on your computer if you were not able to get printed copies of them.

There are several types of printers, the cheapest and most common being a *dot matrix printer*.

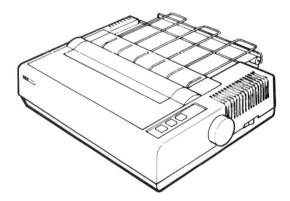

The printing head of a dot matrix printer has a block of *pins*. These look like tiny rods and they create characters with a dot pattern by hammering the correct pins against a ribbon and the paper.

Another type of printer is the *daisy wheel printer*, which works like an ordinary typewriter. Character sets are supplied on metal or plastic *print wheels*, and these can be interchanged to produce different styles of type. Thus, a typical office might have a Letter Gothic print wheel whose results look like they were done on a typewriter, and a Script type wheel that gives a more informal, personal look. The print quality is better than a dot matrix printer, but a daisy wheel printer works much slower and is more expensive.

Users who are preparing documents that have to display the utmost in quality will use a *laser printer*, which gives sharp, crisp images both for text and pictures. However, these are many times more expensive than dot matrix printers and most daisy wheels. But they're quieter and do a better job than any other kind of printer.

Ink jet printers work by shooting a fine jet of ink onto the paper. The newest ink jet printers are as quiet as laser printers and produce results that are comparable in quality. Yet these printers don't cost more than most daisy wheels or heavy-duty dot matrix models. After problems such as clogging and limited types of paper stock have been worked out, look for these units to be the printers-of-choice for those that can't afford lasers.

Programs and Programming Languages

Without instructions or commands, a computer will stand still. With an appropriate set of instructions, a computer can perform many tasks, both simple and complicated. Such a set of instructions is called a *program*. Programs are designed to do specific tasks. The following are the most common types of programs and what they do.

Word Processing	creating texts
Spreadsheets	performing calculations and developing statistical models
Databases	storing and retrieving information
Desktop Publishing	creating brochures & camera-ready copy with text and graphics
CAD	making complex engineering drawings
Communications	allowing your computer to communicate with others

Graphics	creating statistical displays
Accounting	doing invoicing, checkbook balancing, etc.

When creating programs, different *programming languages* can be used. The normal user will not create programs, but will only use commercial programs developed by professional programmers. When running a program, it is not even apparent to the user which programming language has been used to create that program, but here is a list of the more common languages used with PCs in case you have heard them mentioned and wondered what they were:

- C
- Basic
- Pascal
- Assembly Language
- Prolog

There are in fact several hundred different languages. Each language has its own predefined set of commands, and a set of rules on how each command can be used.

DOS

DOS is short for *Disk Operating System*. It's a collection of programs that provide you with a set of commands designed to help you gain access to your hard or floppy disk, and perform some other basic routines. All computers must have such an operating system. When you start your computer, this operating system is automatically loaded into memory.

For example, DOS commands can be used to investigate the contents of a disk, to copy or delete *files*, or to prepare a new floppy disk for use.

DOS is discussed in much greater detail in subsequent chapters.

Files

Many different sorts of information can be stored on a floppy or hard disk. For example, a letter, a word processing program, a diagram, a game program, a programming language, or an address list can all be maintained on a disk. Each complete unit of information is called a file, and has its own unique name.

Filenames can consist of up to eight characters, followed optionally by a period and up to three more characters, for example:

TEST
LETTER1
LETTER2.TXT
CHESS.EXE
CBTEST.EXE

Filenames are covered more thoroughly in Chapter 3.

What Can a Computer Do?

We have already hinted at the different tasks which a computer can perform. This section contains some more general information on the most common uses. First however, here's a summary of the four most basic things a computer can do:

- receive information
- process information
- send out information
- store information

By information we mean text, numbers, pictures, and even electrical voltage. It is the combination of these four processes, controlled with the help of programs, which allow computers to be so versatile.

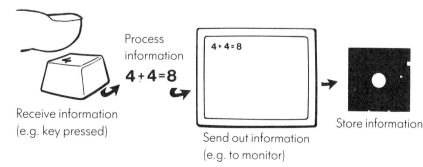

Process information
$4+4=8$

Receive information
(e.g. key pressed)

Send out information
(e.g. to monitor)

Store information

Writing

The most common use for a computer is writing. You can create letters and messages or write entire books. To write with a computer, you generally use a word processing program, although some other kinds of programs can also be used.

After you type in your text, you can save a copy on a disk. Texts are easily edited by inserting and deleting words, or moving sentences and paragraphs around at will. When you make mistakes, you just correct them without ever having to start again, as would be necessary with a typewriter.

Drawing

You can use your computer to create diagrams, pictures, and technical drawings. This sort of work usually requires a large RAM-type memory and a hard disk.

Mouse

An important extra when drawing is a *mouse*. This is a small object which you move around on your desk. As you move it, a "televised" arrow points out where on your screen you are currently aiming.

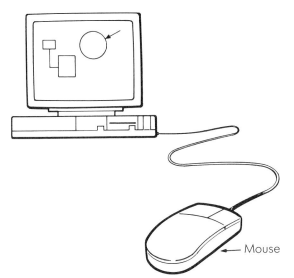

Mouse

Just click one of the mouse's buttons and the cursor will appear at that point. If you're moving the cursor around your screen a lot (as when you're drawing), the mouse is a lot faster than trying to maneuver the cursor using the arrow keys on the computer.

A mouse can also be used with some word processing and spreadsheet programs, and it's required by several of the better desktop publishing programs.

Calculating

A computer can perform calculations very easily and quickly. It takes just a matter of seconds for a computer to count up to 1 million, a feat which a mortal human would have great difficulty doing at all.

Spreadsheet programs help you to organize numerical data for calculation. The numerical grid that a spreadsheet produces is sometimes called a *model*. Results from one part of the model can be used in other parts. By changing certain entries, you can test different assumptions and produce the "what if?" models prized by financial analysts and business school professors.

Database

Database programs allow you to systematically organize and store information on – for example – companies, products, or collectors' items such as records, wine, or stamps. The information is immediately retrievable, and can give you useful lists and analyses. In addition, the better database management programs are so sophisticated that they can be used to do almost anything a computer can do. Increasingly they're being used in place of traditional programming languages to do a wide variety of tasks.

Desktop Publishing

Desktop publishing is the art of producing brochures, manuals, books, and the like on your computer. Such programs allow you to combine text and pictures, and to define the layout and styles used.

You can produce complete works or camera-ready originals that will be sent to a printer. Their most treasured feature is called *WYSIWYG*, which stands for "What You See Is What You Get." This refers to these programs' ability to show multiple fonts, different print sizes and even proportional spacing on the computer screen so that the author can tell exactly what the finished printed copy will look like.

Communications

Communications programs allow you to connect your computer to other computer systems. You can, for example, search for information in many of the available databases, or send and receive mail and files.

Accounting

Many companies use computers for doing all of their accounting functions. Next to word processing, this is probably the most popular application for which personal computers are used in the workplace. Even in major corporations which have giant mainframe systems to do their "official" accounting, many middle managers maintain their own accounting systems on PCs so that they can better keep track of the funds they have spent and have yet to receive.

Graphic Presentations

Another group of programs is aimed at those wishing to produce graphic presentations of statistical results. These are typically produced in the form of charts or overhead transparencies that can be used at meetings.

Industrial Production

Some companies have installed computer systems which control production lines in factories, and programs which help to design products. The latter are called *CAD programs*, which stands for Computer Assisted Drawing or Computer Aided Design.

Playing Games

Most people will try a game program at some time and some of you will get addicted. There are many different sorts of games: adventure games, action games, flight simulators, chess, and sports games, to name but a few.

Kinds of Computers

While all computers can essentially do the same things, the speed and versatility with which they run depends on what type of *processor* they're built around. The processor is the part of the computer which controls all other parts. There are four main processors used in IBM PCs and compatibles. In order of effectiveness, with the slowest and most limited first, they are the *8088*, *80286*, *80386*, and *80486*.

An ordinary PC machine has an 8088 processor and no hard disk. It is a comparatively slow machine by modern standards and it can't run many of the newer programs that require hard disks.

An XT machine has a hard disk, but in other respects is like an ordinary PC.

An AT machine has an 80286 processor which makes it quicker and more powerful than a PC or XT. These machines are almost always equipped with a hard disk and they can run almost all of the programs available today.

Finally, 386 and 486 machines have the even faster 386 and 486 processors. These are the machines power users dream about. A 386 with 2 megs of RAM and a 130 meg hard disk is not considered unusual. Also, these machines are specifically designed to multi-task, which means to run more than one program at a time. Thanks to multi-tasking, a power user can be working on a letter with his word processing program while, in the background, his computer is also chugging away at a statistical analysis that might take several hours to complete.

IBM has also launched its PS/2 computer series which is somewhat different in design from the other models, but comes in models that use all 3 of the processors. Thus, their PS/2 Model 25 uses an 8086 processor (a close relative of the 8088) while their PS/2 Model 80 uses an 80386. The PS/2s are mostly compatible with existing programs but use a different set of accessories and add-in circuit boards.

Another area in which computers differ sharply is their display capabilities.

For instance, a monochrome monitor can cost as little as $79 if it is an *MDA design*, meaning that it's monochrome and can't produce pictures or graphics on its screen, or over $2,000 if it's a *high resolution desktop publishing design* with a 20″ screen that can clearly reproduce 2 facing pages of newspaper classified ads at their actual size.

In between these extremes are the popular *HGA designs* which are said to be *Hercules-compatible*. While these are monochrome, they can use shadings of their basic green or amber color to reproduce a wide range of tones. Also, they can reproduce graphic images and they only cost a little more than the bargain basement MDA models. Thus these can be used in place of more expensive and bulky color monitors when minimal graphics capability is needed.

Among the color monitors, the choice is equally wide. At the low end are the *CGA designs* which produce a full range of colors on what are called *RGB monitors*. About 5 years ago these were the state-of-the-art. Now, due to their relatively poor resolution, they're barely considered acceptable.

On the next rung up the ladder are the *EGA designs*. These are finer in resolution than the CGA models and can produce even a wider spectrum of colors. For most people today, they're quite sufficient.

Finally, we come to the *VGA standard*. These are so fine in resolution and shading that it's easy to mistake animated presentations done on them with videotape or film.

In a class by themselves are the *LCD displays* used on laptop computers. These usually *emulate* or make believe that they're CGA monitors, but they're really monochrome displays that use shadings to reproduce the various colors much the same way the HGA monochrome displays do. The older LCD displays were horrible unless lighting conditions were perfect. Now, thanks to what's called *supertwist technology,* and the building of *backlighting* into the better laptop computers, the displays are fairly good. Nevertheless, using these displays for more than about an hour at a time can be considered cruel and unusual punishment.

The display portion of a computer is called its *graphics subsystem.* This usually consists of a circuit board, called an *adapter card,* which is placed in your computer's system unit, and the appropriate monitor. Sometimes it also includes a special software program, called a *driver,* that's used to ensure that the images generated by a program appear properly on the screen.

There are now monitors and adapter cards that can automatically switch between graphic standards. These are called *multisync monitors and adapters,* and they provide you with at least limited insurance that what you buy today won't be obsolete tomorrow.

What kind of monitor should you buy? That depends on your intended uses and your budget. Today there are millions of users who are happily using inexpensive HGA monochrome systems and slightly more expensive CGA color systems.

But, if you can spend a bit more, try to go for an EGA or multisync color system or – if writing and desktop publishing are your game – a smaller desktop publishing monitor. And if cost is no object, by all means go for VGA or one of those handsome 20″ desktop publishing monitors. After all, you deserve them!

This is, of course, an extreme simplification of a market flooded with computers and accessories.

Points To Remember

Parts of a Computer and Accessories:

- Keyboard
  Monitor
  System unit
  Floppy disk
  Hard disk
  Disk drive
  Printer
  Programs
  DOS
  Mouse

A Computer's Four Functions:

- Receiving information
  Processing information
  Sending out information
  Storing information

- A computer is a very fast, but stupid, electrical appliance.

- It is the multitude of programs that allow the computer to be used for so many different tasks.

- Each unit of information, stored on a disk, is called a file.

Starting Your Computer

Chapter 2   This chapter describes in detail how to start your computer. The assumption is made that it's properly installed and all the cables have been connected correctly.

If your system does not have a hard disk, you will need to have the following item ready for use:

  • Your SYSTEM disk (sometimes called the DOS disk).

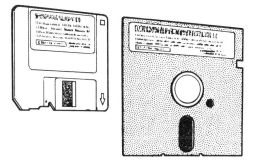

Useful Information Before You Start
Drive A

When starting a computer without a hard disk, you will need to put your DOS disk in drive A. If you have two drives, one on top of the other, the upper drive is usually drive A. If they are side by side, then the left-hand drive is normally drive A.

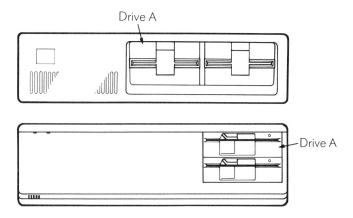

If you only have one floppy disk drive, then your computer is able to pretend that you have two by switching the identity of the drive between A and B, as necessary. When you start your computer the drive will automatically be given the "A" identity.

Right Side Up

When putting a floppy disk into a drive, there are eight different ways of doing it, seven of which are wrong!

● The label on the disk should be on the top side and nearest to you.

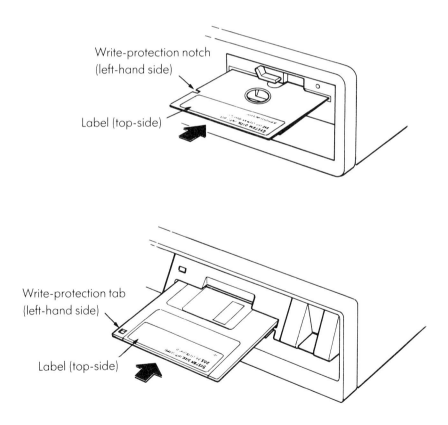

Write-protection notch
(left-hand side)

Label (top-side)

Write-protection tab
(left-hand side)

Label (top-side)

With both kinds of disks the write-protection notch should be on the left-hand side.

If you put the disk in the wrong way, your computer will not be able to use it. A message will be shown on your screen that will say that the disk is not ready for use. If this happens, just take the disk out and put it back in the right way.

Starting the Computer

Your monitor will either get its power from the system unit of the computer or directly from an electrical outlet. In both cases, you will need to check that the power switch to the monitor is turned on.

● Switch on your monitor.

If your monitor gets its power from the system unit, nothing will happen at this point.

● If your computer is a floppy-based system (i.e., no hard disk) place your DOS (or system) disk in drive A, making sure it is the right way and that the drive is closed properly.

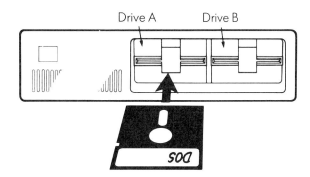

● Switch on your computer.

What happens next depends on your computer and how it is set up. The remainder of this section describes, in general terms, what will happen.

Self-test

The computer will run a quick self-test to check that all of its parts are functioning properly. This may take as little as ten seconds or as much as a minute, depending on the sort of computer you have and the size of its RAM memory.

If any of the parts show a fault, a message will be displayed and the computer may not work. If this happens, switch everything off and start again. If you can't get the computer running after the second or third time, you will need the assistance of a more experienced user.

Load System Files

You will notice some activity from drive A (or your hard disk if you have one). This activity is the necessary system files being automatically loaded into your computer where they are stored in RAM memory.

Some sort of text will also be displayed on your screen, but it is impossible to say just what the message(s) will be, as there are so many possibilities.

Date

One possibility is that you will be asked to confirm the current date.

Note:
This is more usual for a PC type machine. XT, AT and 386 machines normally have an internal clock system with a battery back-up, to keep track of the actual time and date, and therefore do not require such a confirmation.

```
Current date is Thu 01-01-1980
Enter new date (mm-dd-yy):
```

You have two choices. Either confirm the displayed date, or enter the current one. This date will be used by some programs to save you the trouble of entering the date manually, and by others as your computer records when files are saved.

To confirm the displayed date, do the following:

- Press the ↵ key.

To enter your own date, do the following:

- Type in the desired date, for example:

  08-18-88

- Press the ↵ key.

Time

If you were asked about the date, you will probably also be asked about the time.

```
Current time is 08:17:35:26
Enter correct time:
```

You have the same two choices; either confirm the displayed time, or enter a different time.

To confirm the displayed time, do the following:

- Press the ↵ key.

To enter a new time, do the following:

- Type in the desired time, for example:

  19:18

Note that it is sufficient to give only the hour and the minutes.

- Press the ↵ key.

Start a Program

It may happen that your computer automatically starts a program or, for example, a menu system. It will not do this if it has not been specifically programmed to do so.

The System Prompt

Unless another program is automatically started, the *system prompt*, or *DOS prompt*, will be shown on your screen. This can differ from computer to computer, depending on whether you have a hard disk, and if your machine has been programmed to give a special system prompt. The three most likely system prompts are shown below:

```
A:>
```

```
C:>
```

```
C:\>
```

If someone was a bit creative in setting up your computer, the system prompt might also tell you the time and/or the date. In any case, the system prompt is the computer's way of telling you that it is waiting for you to give it a command.

The Cursor

The cursor is a blinking line (–) which shows you where the next thing you type will be positioned on the screen. You will see the cursor together with the system prompt, or while running a program that requires input from you. The form of the cursor may sometimes change into a solid box (■), and the rate at which it blinks may also change.

Restarting Your Computer

It is possible to re-start (otherwise called *boot*, *re-boot*, or *reset*) your computer without switching anything off. If you do this, everything currently stored in the computer's memory will disappear for good, so it can be a rather drastic step to take.

- Some computers will have a reset button, in which case you just press it.

- Some computers allow you to reset by turning a keyboard locking key to a certain position.

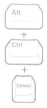

- Another way is by depressing the following three keys at the same time: **Alt** + **Ctrl** + **Del**. Sometimes this method will not work, however, and you may have to switch everything off.

Switching Off

There is nothing complicated about switching your computer off. Just make sure that you have saved any work you have done and then turn it off.

Some Important Beginnings

Chapter 3 This chapter explains some of the most basic ideas and commands which are of great importance for the beginner. For the first time you will be making use of either the optional MASTER floppy disk that came with this book, or a disk called the MASTER that you should create now following the directions in Appendix F.

This chapter concentrates on the floppy disk user. If you have a hard disk, you should still follow this chapter as it contains vital information, and even hard disk users sometimes need to use floppy disks.

Thorough knowledge of the commands covered in this chapter is necessary to be able to fully understand the exercises and explanations in the chapters that follow.

To follow this chapter in its entirety, you will need the following floppy disks:

- Your system or DOS disk (only if you do not have a hard disk).

- Your MASTER program disk.

- Two other disks which can either be new or used. If they've been used before, be sure they do not contain any files that you want to keep.

MASTER Disks

The first golden rule is never to work with MASTER disks. It is not possible to predict when a disk will get damaged as they're really quite fragile. If you have made a copy of a MASTER disk and the copy gets damaged, then you can always go back to the MASTER and make a new copy. If a MASTER disk gets damaged, then that's it — no more programs or files!

Most programs come with an automatic or semiautomatic installation program which helps you to install the program on another disk or on your hard disk. This eliminates the need to make a special copy of the MASTER, as it is done for you.

Sometimes you will just have to use your MASTER disk! When installing a program for the first time, you cannot avoid using it. Indeed, some of the exercises in this book require you to copy files from your MASTER disk. There is one precaution you can take, however, to minimize the small risk of the MASTER being damaged during this process: that is *write-protection*.

Write-protecting disks

Write-protection is a way of preventing your computer from writing data onto a disk, thereby avoiding the possibility of damaging other data already on the disk. This is only a very small risk, but if it happens to you just once, with a disk full of your most precious writings or figures . . .!

The two main uses for write-protection are to protect your MASTER disks and to protect disks which contain important information, such as archive copies of documents and statistics, from being accidently erased.

- Write-protect your MASTER disk now, according to the instructions given below.

5.25" Disks

A 5.25" disk has a write-protect notch on the right-hand side, if you hold it with the label facing you.

- Cover the notch with one of the labels that come with every box of new disks, or with a piece of opaque tape.

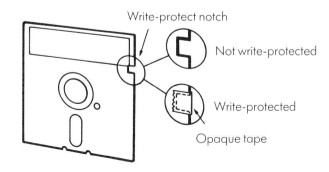

Write-protect notch

Not write-protected

Write-protected

Opaque tape

With the write-protect notch covered, your computer will not be able to write any data on the disk. It will, however, still be able to read the existing data so that you can use or make copies of the files on it.

3.5" Disks

A 3.5" disk has a square write-protect hole with a sliding tab on the right-hand side, if you hold it with the label facing you.

● Move the tab, so that there is a hole right through the disk.

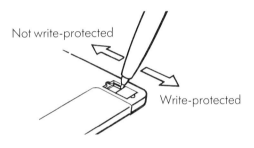

With the write-protect tab open, your computer will not be able to write any data on the disk. It will, however, still be able to read the existing data, so that you can use and make copies of the files on it.

Error Message

You can not add information to a disk that is write-protected. If you are running a program which tries to do so, you will get an error message on your screen, for example:

```
Write protect error writing drive A
Abort, Retry, Ignore?
```

If this happens, you have three choices:

- If you really want to add to the protected disk, then remove the write-protection feature, replace the disk in the relevant drive, and press **R** (= Retry) followed by the ←┘ key.

- Put another disk in the relevant drive, and press **R** (= Retry) followed by the ←┘ key.

- Abandon the procedure by pressing **A** (= Abort) followed by the ←┘ key.

The **I** (= Ignore) choice is not recommended here.

A Little About DOS

DOS is mainly a collection of small programs, often referred to as commands, which help you to save information on disks, and to read that information back into the computer's memory. It can also help you to see the contents of a disk, or to prepare a disk for use.

Internal and External DOS Commands

Basically, there are two classes of DOS commands: *internal* and *external*.

Internal commands are a group of DOS commands which are automatically loaded into your computer's memory when you start it up. These commands remain in memory at all times, and are readily available to the user. They are the most commonly used commands, therefore it is convenient to have them in memory.

External commands are the remaining DOS commands, which are not loaded into the computer's memory. They are stored on your DOS, or system disk, or in a special area on your hard disk. External commands are loaded into the computer's memory only when they are directly called for, and remain in memory only until the relevant task is completed.

The main effect of external commands is that a floppy disk-based computer will require that you insert the DOS disk into one of the drives in order to run such a command.

The Current Drive

Your computer may have just one floppy disk drive, or two, or one or two plus a hard disk, or more than one hard disk, and so on. As mentioned earlier, each drive will be given its own name, such as A:, B:, C:, etc.

When working with DOS commands, you will always be doing something with a file in a specific drive. DOS commands will involve a drive name, and a filename. The concept of a *current drive*, however, provides a useful short cut. In fact it is a little more complicated than that. If you make a mistake, DOS can assume, for example, that you wanted to do something with a file on the current drive, when you really meant another drive and forgot to name it.

The current drive concept is very important to grasp. A normal DOS command, with a specified drive and filename, can be shortened to only a filename, whereupon DOS will assume that the omission of the drive name means that the current drive name is to be used by default. Some exercises which follow later on in this book will use this concept.

You can change the current drive, when the system prompt is shown, by just typing in the drive letter, followed by a colon (:), then pressing the ↵ key.

a: will change the current drive to drive A.

b: will change the current drive to drive B.

c: will change the current drive to drive C.

Another Error Message

```
Disk in drive A not ready . . .
Abort, Retry, Ignore?
```

This will occur when changing the current drive to drive A, if the disk there is either faulty, inserted the wrong way, not properly prepared for use (explained later on in this chapter), or if the drive is not properly closed. As before, you can either remedy the situation and choose to Retry, or you can Abort the process all together.

The DIR Command

The DIR command (DIR is short for directory) will give you a list of contents for a specified disk. DIR is an *internal DOS command*, which means that it is readily available from the computer's memory.

Let's have a look at the contents of your MASTER disk.

- Make sure that you have write-protected your MASTER disk.

- Start your computer, as explained in the previous chapter.

At this point, you should wait for the system prompt to be shown on your screen.

- Put your MASTER disk in drive A.

- Type the following, not missing the space after the command dir:

  `dir a:`

- Press the ← key.

Your computer will now follow the instruction to report the content of the disk in drive A. A list of files present will be displayed. It will look something like this:

```
Volume in drive A is PC CC & SG

Directory of A:\
ANOTHER   TXT      ATD       COM        ATDHELP   COM
EXAMPLE   TXT      TEST1     DOC
TEST2     DOC      KNOWTEST  EXE        ATD_001   COM
ATD_002   COM      ATD_003   COM
ATD_004   COM
          11 File(s)      30720 bytes free
```

Information on the size of the files, and the dates when they were created, is also shown, together with some general information about the disk

The general rule for the DIR command is as follows:

Type DIR, followed by a space, then the name of the desired drive with its colon (:) after it. Press the ↵ key.

Some examples would be:

dir a: for list of files stored on the disk in drive A.

dir b: for list of files stored on the disk in drive B.

dir   for list of files stored on the disk in the current drive.

DIR /w

By extending the command with /w, you can see only the filenames in five columns. This is used when you have lots of files on a disk and you want to see as many names as possible at the same time.

- Type the following:

    dir a: /w

- Press the ↵ key.

Your computer will now display the list of files in five columns:

```
Volume in drive A is PC CC & SG
Directory of A:\

ANOTHER   TXT     ATD        COM     ATDHELP  COM     EXAMPLE  TXT     TEST1    DOC
TEST2     DOC     KNOWTEST   EXE     ATD_001  COM     ATD_002  COM     ATD 003  COM
ATD_004   COM     DIR        DIR     DIR      W
        13 File(s)        29696 bytes free
```

Some examples of commands would be:

dir a:/w
dir b:/w
dir c:/w
dir /w

DIR /p

By extending the command with /p, the list will be presented in one column, but with a pause each time the screen is filled. This is also useful if a disk has a large number of files on it.

- Type the following:

    dir a:/p

- Press the ↵ key.

Your computer will now display the list of files in one column again. Looking at the contents of the MASTER disk, you will not notice any difference compared with the DIR command without the /p extension. If, however, you try DIR with one of your own disks, or with your hard disk, you will get a message similar to the following:

```
Press any key to continue
```

- To see more of the list of files, just press any key.

Some examples of commands would be:

dir a:/p
dir b:/p
dir c:/p
dir /p

Printing a Directory

If you have a printer connected to your computer, you can try using the >prn extension. This will send the file list to your printer instead of to the screen.

- Check that the printer is connected, has paper, then switch it on.

- Type the following (note the space after the a:):

    dir a: >prn

- Press the ←┘ key.

Your computer will now print out the list of files.

Some examples of commands would be:

dir a: >prn
dir b: >prn
dir c: >prn
dir >prn

Filenames

Now that you've seen a few filenames, perhaps it's time to give you the rules for filenames.

A filename can be composed of two parts, the actual name and its *extension*. The name is one to eight characters in length. The extension, if it exists, is a period followed by one to three characters. All the following are examples of filenames:

FILE	FILE.EXE	FILE.DOC
TEST.L	TEST.TXT	TEST.COM
XYZ	X132.11	XR2TH76.HU

Do not use the following characters in a filename:

space
exclamation point (!)
single quote (')
double quotes (")
dollar sign ($)
plus sign (+)
asterisk (*)
less than symbol (<)
greater than symbol (>)
equal sign (=)
slash (/)
semi-colon (;)
colon (:),
comma (,)
ampersand (&)
the @ symbol

As a rule, filenames should be relevant to the contents of the file. A file named WKI8Y7, will not help anyone to remember what it is, whereas names such as ORDER12.TXT, ORDER13.TXT, etc., give a hint to their contents. This may not seem important in the beginning, but with time you may well have hundreds of files so why not make it easy for yourself?

Some extensions are accepted standards, for example:

.EXE and .COM	are program files
.TXT	are test files
.DOC	are word processing files
.BAT	are batch files

Don't worry if you don't understand all these terms. By the end of the book you will.

The FORMAT Command

The FORMAT command prepares new disks for use, a process which is called *formatting a disk*. Used disks can be *reformatted*, in which case their contents will be wiped out.

In this section you will format two disks. One of these will be used in DOS command exercises in coming chapters, and the other will be used for making a system copy disk.

The FORMAT command is an *external DOS command*, which means that it is not readily available in the computer's memory. You will need your DOS or system disk, if you don't have a hard disk, to run the FORMAT program. If you have a hard disk, FOR-MAT is normally stored on it.

To format a disk do the following:

- If you do not have a hard disk, put your DOS disk, which should also be write-protected, in drive A.
- Type:

```
format b:
```

Warning!
If you have a hard disk, be sure not to type just format or format c:.
This will format the whole area of the hard disk and ruin all that you
have stored on it.

You have now told the computer to format a disk in drive B:. To avoid immediately formatting any disk in drive B, DOS gives you the following message:

```
Insert new diskette for drive B:
and strike ENTER when ready
```

- Place the disk that you wish to format in drive B.
- Press the ⏎ key.

The computer will now proceed with formatting. When the process is complete, the following message will be shown:

```
Format another (Y/N)?
```

- Press the **N** key to choose not to format another disk just now.

- Press the ↵ key.

Possible Problems

When trying the FORMAT command, you may get the message:

```
Bad command or filename
```

This is DOS telling you that it can not find the FORMAT command. The most common cause for this is that DOS is looking in the current drive, while you wanted it to be looking somewhere else.

Try changing the current drive to drive A, if you are using a disk based system, or to drive C if you have a hard disk. Retype the FORMAT command, following the instructions as before.

Systems with only one floppy drive, will sometimes get the following message:

```
Insert disk for drive A and strike
any key when ready . . .
```

or:

```
Insert disk for drive B and strike
any key when ready . . .
```

This is because, even if you only have one floppy drive, DOS can pretend that you have two, and change drives when necessary. DOS cannot, however, know which disk you want to be in the current drive, and therefore it gives you the above messages to allow you to change disks as needed.

FORMAT /s

The /s extension to the FORMAT command is very special. It formats a disk and then copies the system files to it. This means that the disk becomes a system disk, and can be used to start your computer.

To format a system disk do the following:

* If you do not have a hard disk, then put your DOS disk, which should be write-protected, in drive A.

* Type:

```
format a:/s
```

You have now told the computer to format a disk in drive A:, and to make it into a system disk. The rest of the procedure is the same as for the plain FORMAT command.

To avoid immediately formatting any disk in drive A, DOS gives you the following message:

```
Insert disk for drive A...
strike ENTER when ready
```

* Place the disk that you wish to format in drive A.
* Press the ↵ key.

The computer will now proceed with formatting. When the process is complete, the following message will be shown:

```
System copied
Format another Y/N?_
```

* Choose not to format another disk.

Note:

If your computer has only one disk drive, or two of the same sort, you will have formatted two diskettes of the same size. If your computer has a 5.25" drive as drive A, and a 3.5" drive as drive B, you will have formatted one diskette of each kind.

Label Your Disks

To keep track of your disks, it is always a good idea to label them. You have now formatted two disks and can write labels for them. Try to write the label before sticking it onto the disk, to avoid pressing with the pen into the disk.

- Label the system disk as:

- Label the nonsystem disk as:

Copying and Deleting Files

Chapter 4   This chapter describes two of the most important DOS commands: those that help you to copy and delete files. You will start by copying the example files from your MASTER disk to the EXER- CISE disk that you formatted in the previous chapter. Make sure that the MASTER disk is write-protected before proceeding with this chapter.

If you have a hard disk, you should still follow this chapter, because it contains invaluable information and useful exercises.

The chapter is divided into two main sections, each covering one of the two DOS commands. Each section has two parts: one describing the command in general terms and one containing exercises to be followed using the step-by-step instructions. If, during the exercises, you get an error message from DOS, you should check **Appendix C.** *Some Common DOS Error Messages* for an explanation of what's happening.

The COPY Command

The COPY command allows you to copy files back and forth between floppy disks and between floppy disks and hard disks. It is an internal DOS command. This means that it is readily available whether or not the system disk containing all of the DOS programs is in your computer.

There are many ways of writing, or abbreviating, the information in a COPY command. But, in this chapter you will learn one general method which always works.

General Rule

The COPY command is made up of the following three parts:

- The command. The word COPY followed by a blank space to separate the command word from the following file information.

- The source. The name of the file to be copied, including information on where it can be found, i.e., on which drive. This is also followed by a blank space to separate it from the next bit of file information.

- The target. The name that the copy should be given along with the name of the drive to which it should be copied.

  COPY From where To where

Some examples would be the following:

copy a:file1 b:filex

This causes the computer to look on the *source disk* placed in drive A for the file named FILE1. If it finds it, then it will make a copy of the file on the *target disk* in drive B, and give the copy the name FILEX. If the file can not be found on drive A, or if for some reason the file can not be copied to drive B, then the process will fail. You'll then get a message saying that no copy was made.

copy b:test.txt a:info.txt

This causes the computer to look on the source disk placed in drive B for the file named TEST.TXT. If it finds it, then it will make a copy of the file on the target disk in drive A, and give the copy the name INFO.TXT.

copy a:happy.txt a:merry.txt

This causes the computer to look on the disk placed in drive A for the file named HAPPY.TXT. If it finds it, it will make a copy of the file on the same disk in drive A. In this case, the same disk is both the source and the target.

Important Considerations

Here are some important points to note:

- You can not have more than one file with the same name on any disk.

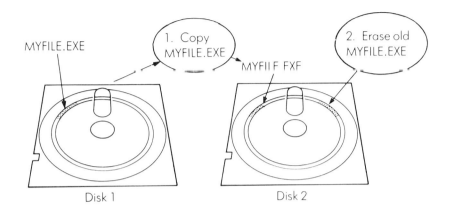

Disk 1   Disk 2

- If you make a copy of a file, and a file of the same name already exists on the target disk, then DOS will *write over* the original copy, in effect erase it, and you will lose the original file on the target disk. This will happen without any prior warning from DOS.
- If you are making a copy of a file on the same disk as the original, you must give the copy a different name.

More About COPY

The information given here about COPY is quite enough for the beginner. The exercises which follow will help you to understand what you have read. The COPY command is explained further in Chapter 5. If you have a hard disk, the COPY command is also discussed again in Chapter 6.

Exercises On the COPY Command

This section contains exercises with step-by-step instructions.

Preparations

In this section, we want you to start your computer by using the newly formatted system disk which you prepared in the previous chapter with the FORMAT A:/S command. If you followed the labeling instructions, this will be your SYSTEM COPY disk. This even applies if you have a hard disk.

- Insert your SYSTEM COPY disk in drive A.

- Start your computer. If it is already running, you should reboot it with **Alt** + **Ctrl** + **Del**, or by using the reset function on your computer. This was explained at the end of Chapter 2.

The system prompt A> will be displayed on your screen when your computer is ready for use.

- Remove the SYSTEM COPY disk from the drive.

Extra Information For Single Disk Drive Computers

If your computer only has one disk drive, you should carefully note the following information:

Your computer will pretend that it has two disk drives, drive A, and drive B, and will actually keep changing the name of the one drive you have. However, to keep up with this name changing, you will have to swap the source and target disks as necessary.

Messages similar to the following, will be displayed at the appropriate times:

```
Insert disk for drive A and strike
any key when ready
```

```
Insert disk for drive B and strike
any key when ready
```

Exercise 1

In this exercise, you will copy files from your MASTER disk to your EXERCISE disk.

- Insert your MASTER disk in drive A. Note that for single disk drive computers, when asking for the disk for drive A, the computer refers to the MASTER disk.

- Insert your EXERCISE disk in drive B. Note that for single disk drive computers, it is not possible to do so at this point. However, when asking for the disk for drive B, the computer refers to the EXERCISE disk, which should then be inserted at the appropriate times.

- Type the following:

```
copy a:test1.doc b:test1.doc
```

- Press the ←┘ key.

The computer will now search the source disk in drive A for the file named TEST1.DOC and make a copy of it on the target disk in drive B, giving the copy the same name. If your computer has only one disk drive, you will have to change disks, as described above.

When the copying is successfully completed, DOS will display the following message:

```
1 File(s) copied
```

The system prompt A> will be shown again, and you may continue.

- Type the following:

```
dir b:
```

- Press the ←┘ key.

This will display a list of files on the disk in drive B and you will be able to see that your file has been copied.

```
TEST1    DOC
```

The system prompt A> will be shown again, and you may continue.

• Type the following:

  copy a:test2.doc b:new2.doc

• Press the ⏎ key.

The computer will now search the disk in drive A for the file named TEST2.DOC and make a copy of it on the disk in drive B. It will give the copy the name NEW2.DOC. If your computer has only one disk drive, you will have to change disks again, as described above.

After completion the system prompt A> will be shown again and you may continue.

• Type the following:

  dir b:

• Press the ⏎ key.

This will display a list of files on the disk in drive B, and you will be able to see that the second file has been copied.

```
TEST1    DOC
NEW2     DOC
```

The system prompt A> will be shown again and you may continue.

• Type the following:

  copy a:example.txt b:new2.doc

- Press the ↵ key.

The computer will now search the disk in drive A for the file named EXAMPLE.TXT and make a copy of it on the disk in drive B, giving the copy the new name NEW2.DOC. Remember, the file NEW2.DOC already exists on your EXERCISE disk (in drive B), but this file will be replaced without warning, by the new file you are copying, with the same name.

After completion, the system prompt A> should be shown again so you may continue with the next command to see what happened.

- Type the following:

      dir b:

- Press the ↵ key.

This will display a list of files on the disk in drive B, and you will be able to see that the third file has been copied, but that it has replaced the second file which had the same name. Therefore, there are not two files named NEW2.DOC on the disk.

```
TEST1    DOC
NEW2     DOC
```

Exercise 2

In this exercise, you will copy a file to the same disk.

- If it is not already there, insert your EXERCISE disk in drive B. If you only have one disk drive, then do not do so at this point.

- Type the following:

      b:

- Press the ↵ key.

This will make drive B the current drive. If you only have one disk drive, you will get the message to insert the disk for drive B. Do so, and then press any key to continue.

The system prompt B> will appear and you may continue.

- Type the following:

  copy b:funny.txt b:extra.doc

- Press the ↵ key.

As you probably have guessed, there is no file named FUN-NY.TXT on the disk, so you will get an error message:

```
File not found
  0 file(s) copied
```

The system prompt B> will be shown again and you may continue.

- Type the following:

  copy b:test1.doc b:extra.doc

- Press the ↵ key.

The computer will now search the disk in drive B for the file named TEST1.DOC, and make a copy of it on the disk in drive B giving the copy the new name EXTRA.DOC.

After completion the system prompt B> will be shown, and you may continue with the next command to see what happened.

- Type the following:

  dir b:

- Press the ↵ key.

This will display a list of files on the disk in drive B, and you will be able to see that the file has been copied.

```
TEST1    DOC
NEW2     DOC
EXTRA    DOC
```

The system prompt B> will be shown again and you may continue.

- Type the following:

  copy b:extra.doc b:extra.doc

- Press the ↵ key.

This doesn't work! You can't have two files with the same name on the same disk, and DOS will refuse to replace a file with itself.

```
File cannot be copied onto itself
```

Exercise 3

Finally, you will use the current drive concept to shorten a copy command like the ones in the previous exercise.

- Type the following:

  copy test1.doc newtest.doc

- Press the ↵ key.

Here the drive name for both files has been omitted, forcing the computer to search the current drive for the source file, and to place the copy file on the current drive with its new name.

After completion the system prompt B> will be shown, and you may continue.

- Type the following:

  dir b:

- Press the ←┘ key.

This will display a list of files on the disk in drive B, and you will be able to see that the file has been copied.

```
TEST1     DOC
NEW2      DOC
EXTRA     DOC
NEWTEST DOC
```

You've completed the COPY exercises, and congratulations are in order. But don't turn off your computer or your mind; you've got one more topic to master in this chapter: deleting files.

The DEL Command

The DEL command allows you to *delete* or *erase* files from floppy and hard disks. Soon you'll be the proud owner of too many unwanted files and a clean-up will be necessary. DEL is an internal DOS command, meaning you do not need your DOS or system disk.

General Rule

The DEL command is made up of the following two parts:

- The command word DEL, followed by a blank space to separate it from the following file information.

- The name of the file to be deleted, including where it can be found, i.e., in which drive.

Some examples would be:

del a:filex
> This causes the computer to look for the file FILEX on the disk in drive A and delete it.

del b:fileq
> This causes the computer to look for the file FILEQ on the disk in drive B and delete it.

Before we go to the exercises, here's some additional information that most experienced users don't even know:

Note!

While the DEL command appears to wipe out the deleted file, in reality only the first character of the file's name is actually destroyed. This causes the file's name to disappear from your disk's directory, but all the data actually remains! I'm telling you this because at some time you'll make a mistake and delete a file that shouldn't have been deleted. When this happens to you, it is often possible, with the right software, to recover a deleted file.

When you find yourself in this position, the important thing is DON'T KEY IN ANY MORE COMMANDS TO THE COMPUTER, DON'T REBOOT IT, AND DON'T TURN IT OFF! If you can keep your head and remember this, you can then ask someone with greater computer knowledge and the proper software to help you save your file, and maybe your job!

Exercise 4

In this exercise, you will remove all the example files on your EXERCISE disk.

- If it is not already there, insert your EXERCISE disk in drive B. If you only have one disk drive, then do not do so at this point.

- Type the following:

    b:

- Press the ←┘ key.

This will make drive B the current drive. If you only have one disk drive, then you will get the message to insert the disk for drive B. Do so, and then press any key to continue.

The system prompt B> will be shown and you may continue.

- Type the following:

  del b:test1.doc

- Press the ↵ key.

This will delete the file TEST1.DOC from the disk in drive B.

After completion the system prompt B> will be shown again, and you may continue.

- Type the following:

  dir b:

- Press the ↵ key.

This will display a list of files on the disk in drive B, and you will see that the file has been deleted, and is no longer listed.

```
NEW2      DOC
EXTRA     DOC
NEWTEST  DOC
```

The system prompt B> will be shown again and you may continue.

- Type the following:

  del b:new2.doc

- Press the ↵ key.

This will delete the file NEW2.DOC from the disk in drive B.

The system prompt B> will be shown again and you may continue.

- Type the following:

  del b:extra.doc

- Press the ↵ key.

This will delete the file EXTRA.DOC from the disk in drive B.

- Type the following:

  del b:newtest.doc

- Press the ↵ key.

This will delete the file NEWTEST.DOC from the disk in drive B.

- Type the following:

  dir b:

- Press the ↵ key.

This will display a list of files on the disk in drive B, and you will see that no files remain.

File not found

You have now completed all the exercises in this chapter.

Points To Remember

- COPY From where To where, for example:

  copy a:filex b:fileq

- DEL This file, for example:

  del b:fileq

- You can not have more than one file with the same name on any disk.

- If you make a copy of a file and a file of the same name already exists on the target disk, then you will lose the original file on the target disk. This will happen without any prior warning from DOS.

- If you are making a copy of a file, and placing the copy on the same disk as the original, you must give the copy a different name than the original.

One Step Further

Chapter 5   This chapter takes you one step further by introducing a new command – TYPE, a new concept – *wild cards*, and by giving you instructions on how to do *screen dumps* and how to get printed copies of files.

Wild Cards

The term *wild card* is, perhaps, a strange term for the high-tech computer world. But just as a joker can be used in place of another playing card in many card games, a wild card can be used in DOS to substitute for any part of a filename.

Wild cards can be used together with many DOS commands, such as DIR, COPY, and DEL, where a filename has to be specified. They allow you to specify groups of files, instead of just single files as we have done so far.

There are two different wild cards, each of which is explained below.

The ? Wild Card

When specifying a filename, you can replace any of the characters in that name with a question mark (?). As an example, assume that you have the following files on your disk in drive B:

    TEST1.DOC
    TEST2.DOC
    FILEQ

Assume also that you want to delete the two files TEST1.DOC and TEST2.DOC. You could delete them one at a time with the following two commands:

```
del  b:test1.doc
del  b:test2.doc
```

However, the ? wild card allows you to delete both files simultaneously with the following command:

```
del b:test?.doc
```

When your computer executes this command, it will delete all files which exactly agree with the specified name, but which have any character instead of the ?. It would, therefore, delete TEST1.DOC and TEST2.DOC.

Now assume that you have the following files on your disk in drive B:

TEST1.DOC
TEST2.DOC
TEST3.DOC
TEST4.TXT
FILEQ

Suppose that you want to delete TEST1.DOC, TEST2.DOC, and TEST4.TXT, but not TEST3.DOC. The same command, that is:

```
del b:test?.doc
```

would not be appropriate, for two reasons. First, TEST1.DOC and TEST2.DOC would be successfully deleted, but so would TEST-3.DOC, which you didn't want to delete. Second, TEST4.TXT would not be deleted, because the extension part of the filename (.TXT), does not match the specified extension (.DOC). In this case, you would have to revert to deleting the files one at a time.

*The * Wild Card*

The * wild card is more powerful than the ? wild card. A * in the specified filename can take the place of any string of characters. You are allowed to have one * wild card in the first part of the filename and one * wild card in the extension part of the name.

Assume that you have the following files on your disk in drive B:

TEST1.DOC
TEST1.BAK
TEST3.DOC
TEST4.TXT
FILEQ.BAK

Suppose you want to delete both files with the extension .BAK, which generally means a backup or duplicate file. You can do this with one command, as follows:

```
del b:*.bak
```

The * can be replaced by any filename, and the only important criteria is that the extension .BAK matches.

Now assume that you have the following files on your disk in drive B:

TEST1.DOC
TEST1.BAK
TEST3.DOC
TEST4.TXT
FILEQ.BAK

This time, suppose you want to delete all files named TEST something, irrespective of their following number or extension. You can do this with one command, as follows:

```
del b:t*.*
```

You are telling the computer to delete all files that begin with a T (remember that the case of a filename is irrelevant) and have any extension.

The *.* file specification

Giving the filename specification *.* is extremely powerful. You are in fact specifying all files with any name and any extension; i.e., all files on the given disk, to be deleted, copied, etc. . . . .

Example 1

```
copy a:*.* b:
```

is a special way of commanding the computer to make a copy of all files on the disk in drive A and placing the copies on the disk in drive B. Notice that no filenames are specified for the copies, thus forcing the computer to give the copies the same names as the original filenames.

Example 2

```
del a:*.*
```

is very effective and dangerous. It commands the computer to delete all files on the specified drive. If you type this command, you will be asked if you are sure about it. This is an automatic safety measure to help you to avoid making mistakes.

Example 3

```
del *.*
```

is likely to cause most users problems sometime in their computer lives. Notice that the drive specification (A: or B:) has been omitted. This is quite all right, but it forces the computer to assume that the appropriate drive is the current drive.

This is where the problem can arise. For example, the user may think he is going to delete all files on the disk in drive B, whereas the computer has other ideas as the current drive is really drive A. You can say bye-bye to all the important files on the disk in drive A unless you've been careful enough to write-protect this disk.

For instance, let's say you've got your $400 word processor master disk in drive A (because you were too lazy to make a working disk as the manual suggested) and you've got your document files from a project you've completed in drive B. You exit your word processor and, because you want to erase all the files on the B disk since you don't need them any more, you type:

```
del *.*
```

What you meant to do was delete all the files on the B disk, but – since you were logged onto drive A when you exited the word processor – what you've really done is delete all the files on that A disk. Then, unless you've got a skilled friend with the proper program standing by, be prepared to call the word processing company and explain how you just wiped out your master disk and want another copy for free.

One way of avoiding this is, especially when using the DEL command, to always specify the drive letter even though DOS doesn't require it. YOU HAVE BEEN WARNED!

Exercise 1

This exercise will help you to understand the wild cards. After each file transfer, use the DIR command to check what has happened. These instructions are not, however, included in the exercises. Refer back to the previous chapters if you need help.

Also, the special instructions about changing disks for users with only one disk drive are now omitted. Again, if you are uncertain about what to do, refer back to the previous chapters. In these exercises, drive A refers to the MASTER disk (apart from the actual start-up of your computer), and drive B refers to the EXER-CISE disk.

Finally, the filenames to be given to copies of files are sometimes omitted. This is deliberate, since it forces the computer to give the copies the same filenames as the original files.

- Start your computer using the SYSTEM COPY disk as explained in the previous chapter.

When the system prompt A> is displayed, you may continue.

- Insert your MASTER disk in drive A.

- Insert your EXERCISE disk in drive B.

- Type the following:

  b:

- Press the ↵ key.

This will make drive B the current drive.

The system prompt B> will be shown, and you may continue.

- Type the following:

  copy a:test?.doc b:

- Press the ↵ key.

This will copy all files on the disk in drive A matching the given filename, but with any single character replacing the ? character, onto the disk in drive B. The copies will have the same filenames as the original files.

- Type the following:

  copy a:*.txt b:

- Press the ↵ key.

This will copy all files on the disk in drive A which have the extension .TXT onto the disk in drive B. The copies will retain the same filenames as the original files.

- Type the following:

  dir b:*.doc

- Press the ↵ key.

This will display a list of all files on the disk in drive B with the extension .DOC.

- Type the following:

  dir a:c*.exe

- Press the ↵ key.

This will display a list of all files on the disk in drive A, which have filenames starting with C, and which have the extension .EXE.

- Type the following:

  copy b:test1.doc b:text1.doc

- Press the ↵ key.

- Type the following:

  del b:tes*.*

- Press the ↵ key.

This will delete all files on the disk in drive B, which start with TES.

And now for the billion dollar command . . .

- Type the following:

  del b:*.*

- Press the ↵ key.

Yes, it's that dangerous command, so you will be prompted to confirm it:

```
Are you sure (Y/N)?
```

- Press the **Y** key to confirm your desire to delete all files on the disk in drive B.

- Press the ↵ key.

You could also have pressed the **N** key, to abort the deletion process.

You have now completed this exercise, and your EXERCISE disk should be empty again. Check this with the DIR command and go on to the next section.

The TYPE Command

The TYPE command gives you a way of looking at the contents of a file. TYPE is an internal DOS command that's readily available.

General Rule

The TYPE command has two parts to it:

- The command. The command word TYPE, followed by a blank space to separate it from the following file name.
- The source. The name of the desired file, including the drive where it can be found.

Exercise 2

- Insert your MASTER disk in drive A.
- Type the following:

  ```
  a:
  ```

- Press the ←┘ key.

This will make drive A the current drive.

The system prompt A> will be shown, and you may continue.

- Type the following:

  ```
  type a:test1.doc
  ```

- Press the ←┘ key.

The contents of the file will be displayed on your screen:

```
Hi there.
This is just one of those boring old example texts.
Bye.
```

On completion, the system prompt A> will be shown again, and you may continue.

- Type the following:

  ```
  type a:test2.doc
  ```

- Press the ↵ key.

The contents of the file will be displayed on your screen:

```
Hi there,
You guessed it, another boring old example text.
Bye.
```

You have now completed Exercise 2.

Using Your Printer

This section assumes that you have a printer connected to your computer, and that it is turned on and ready to run.

Screen Dumps

A screen dump sends a copy of the text displayed on your screen to your printer. If there are graphic displays included in the text, they may or may not print depending on the capabilities of your printer.

To obtain a screen dump, do the following:

- Press the **PrtSc** key.

Note:
Many keyboards require you to press **Shift** *and* **PrtSc**

A copy of the screen display will be printed out on your printer.

Copying Files To a Printer

Just as you used the TYPE command to display the contents of a file on your screen, you can use the COPY command to print out a file.

This command is like the ordinary COPY command, but the third part, or target, is replaced by PRN, which sends the copy to the printer instead of to the disk.

The example in Exercise 3 will help you to understand this command.

Exercise 3

- Insert your MASTER disk in drive A.
- Type the following:

  a:

- Press the ←⏎ key.

This will make drive A the current drive.

- Type the following:

  dir a:

- Press the ←⏎ key.

This will show you the contents of your disk.

- Type the following:

  copy a:test1.doc prn

- Press the ←⏎ key.

A copy of the file TEST1.DOC will be printed.

You have now completed all of the exercises in this chapter.

Points To Remember

- When specifying a filename, you can replace any single character in that name with a question mark (?).
- When specifying a filename, you can replace any part of the name, or extension with an asterisk (∗).
- TYPE This file
- **PrtSc**, or **Shift** + **PrtSc**, for screen dumps.
- COPY SourceFile PRN, to print out a file.

The Secrets of a Hard Disk

Chapter 6

Why do so many people buy hard disks? The answer is simple. Hard disks can store much more information than floppy disks, and they work much faster.

The smallest hard disks generally available today can store 20 million bytes, the equivalent of 10,000 pages. Hard disks which store up to 130 million bytes now come standard with some computers and much larger ones are available at extra cost.

With so much storage space available, a hard disk will often have thousands of different files on it. The secret of a hard disk is . . . well try guessing! How would you like it if every morning you went to your closet to get some clothes, and over a thousand different pieces of clothing lay in one big unsorted heap? Don't you have your shirts in one place, your socks in another, etc.?

This chapter will not help you get dressed in the morning, but it will provide valuable information for the hard disk owner. As with previous chapters, some DOS commands and concepts will be introduced and there are exercises to put them into use.

Even if you don't have a hard disk, reading this chapter can be very useful. You can also follow all the exercises, with the exception of Exercise 3, by putting your exercise disk in drive A (after start-up), and replacing each occurrence of c: in a command, with a: .

Organizing Your Hard Disk

To find any given file among all the files you may have on your hard disk, some sort of organization is needed. The answer is to divide the hard disk into different areas, which are called *directories* in computer language.

A hard disk divided into different directories is a well structured system. You can build this structure to suit your own needs, but it will always contain certain elements.

A hard disk always has one main directory which is called the *root directory*.

When you create new directories, they can be placed directly under the root directory or under any other existing directory. Directories which are positioned under another directory are referred to as *subdirectories*. Consider this example.

First you create three special directories, one each for your word processor, spreadsheet, and database programs.

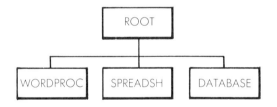

All files connected with your word processor you store in the word processor directory. Then, let's say that you use your word processor for three purposes: business correspondence, private correspondence and creating product information sheets for your business. Since you have lots of files of each type you don't want to get them all mixed up with one another (remember the closet). Therefore, you create subdirectories in your word processor directory where each type of file is stored separately.

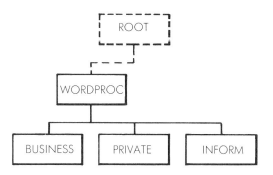

In this way, you can build a hard disk structure to suit your own needs. All files can be placed in a relevant directory, making it much easier to find them when they're needed. The overall structure you create is called a *tree*, and DOS actually has a command called TREE that will permit you to print out the tree structure of your disk.

You can also build the same sort of tree structure on a floppy disk, but because the storage volume is so limited it is usually not necessary.

The Current, or Working Directory

With a structure of directories on your hard disk, your computer needs to know which directory it should be working with. The computer will always stay in the same directory or subdirectory, which is called the *current directory* or the *working directory*, until you tell it to change to another. Thus, it keeps track of the current directory in the same way that it keeps track of the current drive (A, B, C, etc.).

To show the user which directory is the current one, the system prompt can be extended to show the name of the current directory, for example:

```
C: \>
```

```
C: \WORDPROC>
```

```
C: \WORDPROC\PRIVATE>
```

All levels of the current directory are shown.

The Symbol \

In the previous examples, note the backslash (\) symbol being used. This has two different meanings, depending on its position.

When the \ symbol is located directly after the drive name (with its colon), it signifies the root directory. When naming a directory, the computer always starts from the root directory and works down through the tree. Thus, the root directory symbol \ is always shown first. While all other directories have their own specific names, the root directory has the name \.

When used further down the structure, in what's called the pathname, the \ symbol is used to separate the names of the different directories and subdirectories from each other and from the root directory.

The Pathname

In our example, there is a directory named \PRIVATE. This is the actual name of that directory. \PRIVATE is, however, a subdirectory of the \WORDPROC directory, which is itself a subdirectory of the ROOT directory called C:\.

The pathname gives the complete route that the computer will have to travel to find a given directory, starting from the drive name and root directory.

For this example, the actual directory name is PRIVATE, but its pathname is C:\WORDPROC\PRIVATE.

It is possible to have two or more directories with the same name, for example PRIVATE, but their pathnames will be different, e.g.:

    C:\WORDPROC\PRIVATE
    C:\DATABASE\PRIVATE

The PROMPT pg Command

The *extended system prompt*, showing the current directory and its pathname, is just about a necessity for hard disk users. Unfortunately, it's not an automatic feature in DOS. For this reason, your computer has to be instructed to use this prompt with a special DOS command.

If it's not set up for the extended system prompt, the prompt will always be the plain C:> prompt, irrespective of the name of the current directory.

To tell whether your computer is using extended system prompts, just note what the prompt is when you first turn your computer on or reboot it. If the prompt is C:\ (or A:\), then your machine is already set up for extended system prompts. But if the prompt is plain C: (or A:), then it's not.

If your computer is not already displaying extended system prompts, do the following:

- Check that the system prompt C:> is displayed on your screen.

- Type the following:

  `prompt $p$g`

- Press the ↵ key.

The extended system prompt will thereafter be shown until you turn off your computer or reboot it. When you follow the exercises later on, you will use this command.

The CD Command

The CD command stands for *change directory*, and it's used to change to a new current directory.

General Rule

The CD command has two parts to it:

- The actual command word CD, followed by a blank space.

- The name of the desired directory.

Some examples would be:

`cd \`

This changes the current directory to the root directory.

`cd \wordproc\private`

This would change the current directory to the specified directory.

`cd..`

This moves the current directory one step upwards in the directory structure. In our example structure, if the current directory was PRIVATE, the cd.. command would result in WORDPROC becoming the new current directory. Note that in some older versions of DOS, the command cd.. requires a space before the first period. More recent versions of DOS will accept the command without the space.

Considerations

There are two ways to move around a directory structure. You can move up or down one level at a time, or you can move directly to a fully specified directory.

- To move up one level, use the `cd..` command as described above.

- To move down one level, use the CD command together with the name of the new directory, but without giving a full path-name. For example:

```
C:\WORDPROC>cd private
```

would successfully change the current directory to PRIVATE. This shortened command only works, however, if the specified directory exists as a subdirectory to the current one. For example:

```
C:\WORDPROC>cd database
```

This would fail, because the DATABASE directory is not a sub-directory of the WORDPROC directory.

- To move directly to any directory, you can give the complete pathname for that directory.

The MD Command

The MD command stands for *make directory*, and it's used to create directories and subdirectories.

General Rule

The MD command has two parts to it:

- The actual command word MD, followed by a blank space.
- The name of the directory to be created.

Some examples would be:

```
md \database\company
md test
```

Considerations

There are two ways of creating directories.

- By specifying the complete pathname to an already existing directory, and adding the new directory name, you can create a directory anywhere in the tree structure.
- By only specifying the new directory name, you can create the new directory as a subdirectory to the current directory.

The RD Command

The RD command stands for *remove directory*, and it's used to remove directories from your disk.

General Rule

The RD command has two parts to it:

- The actual command word RD, followed by a blank space.
- The name of the directory to be removed.

Some examples would be:

```
rd \database\company
rd test
```

Considerations

There are two ways of removing directories.

- Specify the complete pathname to an existing directory, to delete a directory anywhere in the directory structure.

- Only specify the directory name, and delete the stated directory, providing that it is a subdirectory to the current directory.

A directory may only be removed if it is empty. To be removed successfully, it must contain no files and have no subdirectories of its own.

Exercises – General

The remainder of this chapter contains four exercises, designed to demonstrate these new commands. In order to follow them exactly, you should start your computer using the SYSTEM COPY disk.

- Insert your SYSTEM COPY disk in drive A.

- Start your computer.

The system prompt `A:>` will be displayed when the computer is ready for use.

- Type the following, to make C the current drive:

b) `c:`

- Press the ↵ key.

The system prompt `c:>` will be displayed.

- Type the following, to obtain the extended system prompt:

`prompt $p$g`

- Press the ↵ key.

The system prompt `c:\>` will now be displayed. Notice that the root directory symbol \ has been added to the system prompt.

l

During the following exercises, you will create and work with the following directory structure:

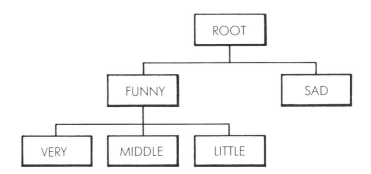

You will also need your MASTER disk again.

Exercise 1

In this exercise, you will create the directory structure above.

Creating Subdirectories

- Type the following to make sure that the root directory is the current directory:

    cd \

- Press the ↵ key.

- Type the following to create the FUNNY directory right under the root directory (i.e., no pathname given):

    md funny

- Press the ↵ key.

- Type the following to create the SAD directory as a direct sub-directory to the root directory (i.e., no pathname given):

    md sad

- Press the ↵ key.

Note:

If you already have one of the above directories on your hard disk, you will get the following error message:

```
Unable to create directory
```

In such an unlikely case, you will have to substitute another directory name for ours throughout the exercises.

This may also occur if you have previously followed these instructions, but haven't removed the directories. In such a case, you may just continue.

Creating Directories Anywhere in the Structure

You will now create directories for VERY and MIDDLE by specifying the complete pathname.

- Type the following:

  ```
  md \funny\very
  ```

- Press the ↵ key.

- Type the following:

  ```
  md \funny\middle
  ```

- Press the ↵ key.

Creating Another Subdirectory

The final directory, LITTLE, will again be created as a subdirectory of the current directory. To place it correctly, you will have to change the current directory to FUNNY. The root directory is the current directory, FUNNY lies directly under it, so you don't have to give any pathname to move down one level.

- Type the following:

  ```
  cd funny
  ```

- Press the ↵ key.
- Type the following:

  md little

- Press the ↵ key.

Exercise 2

In this exercise, you will move around the directory structure with the CD command. The result of each command will be reflected by the system prompt.

Move to the Root Directory

You can always change to the root directory in one simple step. Do the following:

- Type:

  cd \

- Press the ↵ key.

Moving Down One Level at a Time

You can move down in the structure one level at a time just by giving the directory name. This is assuming that the given directory exists as a subdirectory of the current directory. Here we'll change from the ROOT directory, down to FUNNY, then down to MIDDLE.

- Type:

  cd funny

- Press the ↵ key.
- Type:

  cd middle

- Press the ↵ key.

Moving Up One Level at a Time

You can move up one level at a time from a directory to its *parent directory*, the directory directly above it. We will now move from MIDDLE, up to FUNNY, up to ROOT, and down to SAD.

- Type:

  `cd..`

- Press the ↵ key.

- Type:

  `cd..`

- Press the ↵ key.

- Type:

  `cd sad`

- Press the ↵ key.

Moving Directly To Any Directory

You can move directly to any directory by specifying its complete pathname. This method is often used to jump sideways in a directory structure, rather than first upwards and then down again. You will now change from SAD, to LITTLE, then to VERY.

- Type:

  `cd \funny\little`

- Press the ↵ key.

- Type:

  `cd \funny\very`

- Press the ↵ key.

Exercise 3

In this exercise, you will copy files between directories.

- Put your MASTER disk in drive A.

Copying Files to the Current Directory from Another Directory

- Make MIDDLE the current directory by typing:

  cd \funny\middle

- Press the ↵ key.

You will now copy the files from the MASTER disk to the MIDDLE directory.

- Type one of the following:

  copy a:*.* b:\funny\middle

  or:

  copy a:*.*

Notice that these two commands are equivalent. By omitting the target drive and directory in the second command, the computer is forced to assume that you mean the current drive and the current directory. The absence of any filenames for the copies forces the computer to give the copies the same names as the originals.

- Press the ↵ key.

Copying Files from the Current Directory to Another Directory

You will now copy some of the files to the SAD directory.

- Type one of the following:

      copy c:\funny\middle*.doc c:\sad *doesn't WORK*

  or:

      copy *.doc ~~B~~ c:\sad — *WORKS*

Once again, the first command is the complete command. This time we cannot shorten the target information, as we want to copy files to a directory other than the current directory. We can, however, shorten the source information as we are copying files from the current directory. In the absence of directory information for the source, the computer will assume that we mean the current directory. The absence of any filenames for the copies forces the computer to give the copies the same names as the originals.

- Press the ↵ key.

Copying Files from Any Directory to Any Other Directory

You will now copy the files in the SAD directory to the VERY directory, noting that neither of them is the current directory.

- Type the following:

      copy c:\sad*.* c:\funny\very

The absence of any filenames for the copies forces the computer to give the copies the same names as the originals. Neither source directory, nor target directory can be shortened. As drive C is the current drive, you could leave out the drive name in both cases.

Exercise 4

In this exercise you will empty the directories and delete them.

Emptying the Directories

The first stage is to delete all the files that you have copied.

- Type the following:

  `del c:\sad\*.*`

- Press the ↵ key.

- Confirm your wish to delete all files in this directory by pressing **Y** then ↵.

- Type the following:

  `del c:\funny\middle\*.*`

- Press the ↵ key.

- Confirm your wish to delete all files in this directory by pressing **Y** then ↵.

- Type the following:

  `del c:\funny\very\*.*`

- Press the ↵ key.

- Confirm your wish to delete all files in this directory by pressing **Y** then ↵.

Removing a Subdirectory That's Directly Under the Present One

To remove a subdirectory, it must be empty, and it must lie directly under the current directory. To remove the LITTLE directory this way, we must first make FUNNY the current directory. We can then remove the VERY directory (which we will do), and the MIDDLE directory (which we will not do).

- Type the following:

  `cd \funny`

- Press the ↵ key.

- Type the following:

  `rd little`

- Press the ↵ key.

- Type the following:

  `rd very`

- Press the ↵ key.

Removing Any Directory

You can remove any directory, providing it is empty and has no subdirectories, by specifying the complete pathname to that directory.

- Type the following:

  `cd \`

- Press the ↵ key.

- Type the following:

  `rd \funny`

- Press the ↵ key.

You should get the following error message:

```
Directory not empty
```

This is because although it does not contain any files, the FUNNY directory does have one subdirectory, MIDDLE, which must be removed first.

- Type the following:

  `rd \funny\middle`

- Press the ↵ key.

- Type the following:

  `rd \funny`

- Press the ↵ key.

- Type the following:

  `rd \sad`

- Press the ↵ key.

You have now completely removed the structure you built up in these exercises.

How to Sound Like a Techie Even If You Aren't One

Chapter 7 This chapter is designed for people who would like to know more about how a computer works. The language is nontechnical so that anyone who has gotten this far will be able to understand.

The Heart of a Computer

Your heart beats about 70 times each minute. This varies from person to person, but we are all dependant on heartbeats to send oxygen enriched blood through our bodies. A computer has no blood, but it does have a heart-like component. A *clock* inside the computer sends out pulses at regular intervals. Each pulse triggers the execution of an instruction which then flows within the computer from one part to another. The computer is dependent upon the pulses of its clock just as we're dependent upon the beats of our heart.

The clock inside a computer sends out several million pulses per second. The pulse rate differs by model. PCs and XTs have slower rates, ATs and 386 machines are faster.

You may have heard or read such terms as

    12 MHz processor
    25 MHz processor

These terms measure the rate at which the clock is set to permit the *processor* to work, in pulses per second. *25 MHz* is 25 million pulses per second.

The Brains of a Computer

A human brain is very complex, capable of processing the millions of electrical impulses coming from our five senses in a split second. A PC also has a sort of a brain, which controls everything going on within it, at clock rates which currently range from 4 million to 25 million instructions per second. The computer's brain is the *processor.*

Processors for IBM PCs and clones are manufactured by the Intel Corporation, and are given names such as the *8088* (used in plain PC and XT machines), *80286* (used in ATs or 286 machines) and *80386* (used in the 386 machines).

What Happens When You Start Your Computer?

When you switch on your computer, it may take several seconds before it is ready to use. What happens is that the computer starts off with a kind of morning gymnastics routine, checking to see that all parts of its body are ready for the day's work. It automatically runs a *test program* to check that the keyboard, monitor, and other parts are functioning properly.

Next, the computer will automatically load some system information, called BIOS, then the internal DOS commands into its memory. BIOS stands for *Basic Input Output System*, and *DOS* stands for *Disk Operating System.*

The final stage of the computer's warm-up is to look for any file information for which it is pre-programmed to look. This information is given in two special files, CONFIG.SYS and AUTO-EXEC.BAT. Neither is necessary, but both are very common. You can inspect these files by using TYPE to print their contents on the screen if they exist on your system disk. (On a hard disk they will almost certainly exist.)

When all of this is done, the system prompt will be shown along with the cursor. The computer is then ready for your commands.

This may not be the case, however, if you have an AUTO-EXEC.BAT file. This file has the capability to automatically start another program, initiate a menu system which makes the computer easier for novices to use, or to change the way the system prompt or the cursor looks. Thus if your AUTOEXEC.BAT file has been programmed to put you right into the data entry mode of your database manager, or to display a menu with program names on your monitor, you may never see the system prompt.

What Happens When You Press a Key?

When you press a key, a code number for the key pressed is automatically generated. That code number is placed in the *keyboard buffer* which is a kind of waiting room for keyboard code numbers.

Your computer checks at regular intervals – many times a second – to see if any code numbers are waiting to be picked up from the keyboard buffer. If there are, the code number is instantly moved to the computer's processor and assessed. The key stroke is then usually sent to the monitor so that you see which key you have pressed.

Please understand that all this happens in a flash. In fact, your computer spends most of its time waiting for you to press a key!

Character Representation

The computer does not work with keys and numbers, but with electricity and voltage levels. Computer engineers define that a *high voltage* of about 5 volts is equivalent to 1, and a *low voltage* of around 0 volts is equivalent to 0. The 1's and 0's are then gathered into their own code, called *binary*, to represent numbers and letters. It's these binary codes which, in turn, build commands and other information.

Take the letter A, for example. This has been given the decimal code number 65, which translated to 1's and 0's in binary becomes

01000001. Thus, if we have 8 electrical wires in which the voltage levels can be made either 0 or 5, we can represent that letter A by setting the voltages in the second and eighth wires to 5, and setting the others to 0.

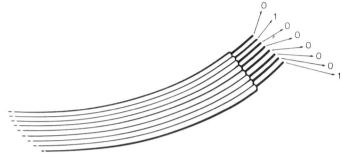

In this way, it is easy to understand that a computer is merely a simple electrical appliance. It deals only with electricity. When you press the A key, an A doesn't appear anywhere in the computer. The manufacturers have only printed an A on the key to make it easier for you. Pressing that key generates a series of electrical voltages. These voltages are then processed within the computer, which in turn generates other voltages which cause your monitor to display the letter A again, by lighting up the necessary dots, or *pixels*, on your screen.

All this happens very, very quickly. If your computer's clock could only generate one pulse per second, instead of several million, it would take several minutes to show the letter A on the screen after you had pressed the A key.

Bits and Bytes

Each single 1 or 0 is called a *bit,* i.e., it is a bit of a complete unit of information. A complete information unit is a group of 8 bits, and is called a *byte.*

Each single bit, within a byte, can take the value 1 or 0. Each letter, number, or graphics character has its own unique bit combination. The letter A is represented by 01000001, the number 7 by 00111001.

When we talk about the size of a computer's memory, we mean how many bytes, or characters, it is capable of storing. One kilobyte (1 kb) is the equivalent of 1024 bytes, so a computer with 640 kb memory can store 1024×640 = 655,360 bytes, or characters.

How is Information Stored?

You can think of a computer's memory as a large cupboard divided into thousands of pigeonholes. One byte of information can be stored in each pigeonhole. This means that to store the word America, 7 pigeonholes would be occupied, one for each letter of the word.

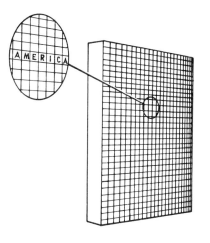

A computer with 640 kb memory, will have 655,360 pigeonholes in its cupboard. It keeps track of what's where, by numbering each hole from 0 to 655,360. When a character is to be stored in memory, it is given a numbered address, and stored accordingly.

What Happens When You Run a Program?

Most of the time you use your computer you will be running programs. When you start a program, a copy of the program is fetched from the relevant disk, and stored in the computer's memory. The original program information remains on the disk, and your computer works only with the information that is copied into its memory.

During the running of the program, different parts of the memory will be used to store information used in that program. The computer automatically keeps track of where it places relevant information.

Your keyboard inputs will be processed, and instructions carried out, as defined in the program. The computer could not do anything without these program instructions.

What Does a Computer Look Like Inside?

If you take the lid off your computer, which is not dangerous to either you or the computer so long as the power cable is disconnected, you will see a lot of green *circuit boards*, full of small black *chips*.

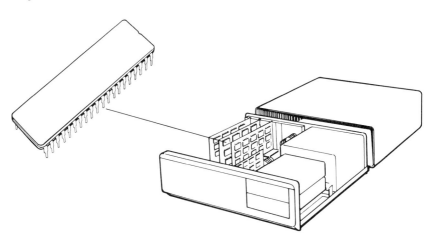

Each chip has its own tasks to perform. Some are memory chips. Others help to process keyboard inputs and the output to the monitor. The largest chip is most often the processor, the computer's brain.

Every chip contains from just a few up to several hundred thousand *transistors*. During manufacture, 95 percent of all chips are thrown away as only a few work properly

Other small components you can see are capacitors, diodes, resistors, and transistors.

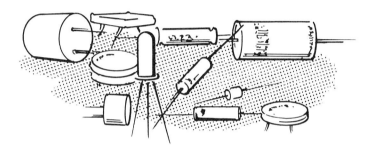

What Is a Disk?

A disk is a plastic wafer that's covered by a thin magnetic film. Information can be stored on disks, rather like on an ordinary musical cassette tape, by magnetizing it in a special way. The thin disk is protected by a thicker plastic jacket.

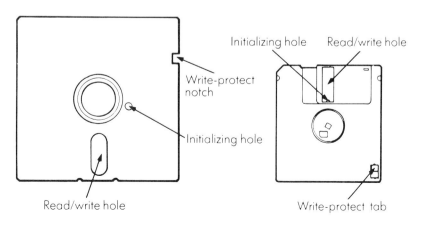

Write-protect notch

Initializing hole

Read/write hole

Initializing hole

Read/write hole

Write-protect tab

The central hole is used by the motor in the disk drive unit to engage and rotate the disk. The larger opening, revealing the actual disk, is where information is read from, and written to, the disk. The very small hole is used as an initializing point for the disk. However, the 3.5″ diskettes do not have an initializing hole in them, rather, they have an extra hole in the metal hub which mates with a key peg on the spindle of the disk drive.

What Is Formatting?

A completely new disk, or hard disk, usually cannot be used without first being prepared for use. This is called *formatting*.

When formatted, the disk is divided up in a special way. Starting from the outside, it's divided into a given number of concentric *tracks*. These tracks are then divided into *sectors*. Some sectors are reserved by DOS to keep a directory of stored files. The rest of the disk is available to store information on. The number of tracks, and the amount of information or *density* that can be stored on each track, determine the storage capacity of the disk.

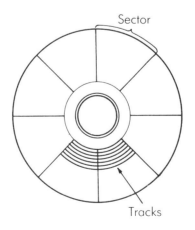

Sector

Tracks

Communications Crash Course

Chapter 8 One of the most exciting aspects of the world of computers is the possibility of communicating with others. Just imagine being in touch, from your home or office, with other users in New York, Rome, Tokyo, or perhaps a remote farm in the deepest forests of Sweden, or any other isolated place!

If you're a beginner in communications, just inquisitive, or one of those who have accepted that communications probably is an exciting possibility, "but why in the world didn't it work for me . . . ?" then you should read this very basic guide.

Why Communicate?

People communicate either because it's fun or because it's necessary. Either way, there are five main areas of communication:

1. Data Transfer

Data transfer involves sending data from one computer to another. Where the two computers are situated is not very important and the data can really be anything: a document or message, a set of financial reports, a picture, a program. Data transfers can be simple messages, or with the help of a specialized communications program, reports can be sent to hundreds of specified destinations at specified times. Computer programs can also be sent from one place to another.

2. Information Retrieval

Around the world are many information services that provide databases through which you can access information and data on just about anything and everything. You can keep up-to-date with Wall Street using data provided by Dow Jones, check the times of flights to Seattle, or scan travel news, books, entertainment, press releases, scientific reports – to name just a few areas. A warning: searching for information can be expensive. If you intend to do a lot of searching, find out the costs first, and get instructions that will help you access the information efficiently.

3. **Control of a Remote Computer**
Together with a specially designed program, it is possible to sit by one computer and control another computer. You can, for example, use a computer at home to work with your office computer, or a computer consultant could help you correct a problem on your computer without having to leave his or her office.

4. **BBS – Bulletin Board Systems**
A BBS is a sort of local communications center to which several users (often hundreds) call to exchange messages, ideas, and programs. Many software houses now have their own BBS acting as a support center for their products.

5. **Direct Contact With Other Users**
You can call another person and be in direct contact with him, thus creating an interactive communications session. You could, for example, exchange ideas and transmit files. There are even on-line computer dating services!

What Do I Need?

Basically you need a communications program, a modem, a serial port on your computer, and a telephone line.

Modem – What's That?

Modem is short for *Modulator/Demodulator*. None the wiser? Well, a telephone line is best suited for a human voice, not for transmission of the sort of data your computer likes to send. A modem, which is connected between your computer and the telephone line, *converts* (modulates) the computer's data signals to more human-like tone signals, which can then be transmitted over the line. Another modem at the other end will receive the call and *re-convert* (demodulate) it to data signals which the receiving computer can understand.

A modem can either be a stand-alone unit connected to your computer's serial port and to a telephone line, or an add-on card which is mounted inside the computer.

The most important feature for a modem is its transmission speed. This is measured in *Baud* or *bps* (bits per second) which are explained further later on in this chapter. A higher Baud rate means a faster transmission and a lower telephone bill, but it also means a more expensive modem. It will be a question of measuring your needs against your means.

Serial Port

A *serial port* is a special sort of connector through which your computer can send data to the outside world, which might happen to be, for example, a modem or a serial printer.

If you have an external modem, i.e., stand-alone modem, it will also have a serial port which has to be connected to a serial port on your computer.

Most computers have one or two serial ports, but it is possible that you will need to buy an extra serial port if, for example, you are using the present one(s) for a serial mouse and/or a serial printer, or some other computer add-on.

A serial port can have 9 or 25 pins. It's easy to check the back of your computer to see if you have a free serial port, but don't mix a 25 pin serial port with a 25 pin parallel port. This is what they look like:

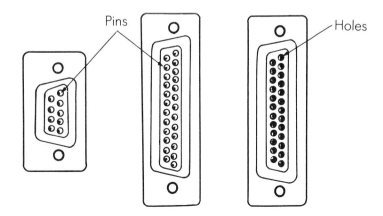

You will have to buy the right sort of cable to connect the modem to your computer. When buying the cable it's important to state that your serial port has 9 or 25 pins and that it is for a modem, as there are other sorts of serial cables designed for other uses.

What's Next?

Assuming that you've correctly installed your modem, and installed and started your communications program, (according to the manual supplied with the program!!!) everything can still go wrong! There are a lot of settings which must be right so as to avoid getting nothing but garbled rubbish, or worse, getting nothing at all.

Some of the most important aspects of communications are explained in the following sections.

Protocol

The word "*protocol*" may sound more difficult than it is. A protocol is merely the collective name given to a set of rules which, when followed, will enable computers to communicate.

Synchronous and Asynchronous Transmission

Synchronous and *asynchronous* transmission relates to the "rhythm" with which data is transferred.

Synchronous transmission implies that data is transferred at a steady rate. Both the transmitting and receiving computers are synchronized at the start of a transfer session and the data is sent at a regular rate. If you feel your pulse (assuming it is regular) you can imagine that data is transmitted at each beat. For a computer, the beats are, of course, much faster – even for those of you who have a fast pulse!

Asynchronous transmission implies that data is transferred at irregular intervals. This means that data can be sent from one computer to another at any time (assuming they are connected). A problem arises here however.

One computer can quite easily send data at any point in time, but the receiving computer has to be ready to accept the data. To prepare the receiving computer for the incoming data, a warning signal is sent to "wake it up." This is called a *start bit*. The actual information bearing data bits follow. Finally a *stop bit* is sent to inform the receiver that the incoming data information has ended.

All of this happens automatically, but the communications programs being run by the two computers must be set up in the same way, that is, set for the same number of data bits (normally 7 or 8) and stop bits (normally 1, sometimes 2).

Parity

Another concept is that of *parity*. Parity is used to check that a data transfer has been completed correctly. Your communications program will allow you to set up even, odd, or no parity. A parity bit is added to each byte sent as a sort of control bit. An example will best explain these terms:

Character	S	a	m
ASCII	1	1	1
Code in	0	1	1
Binary	1	0	0
	0	0	1
	0	0	1
	1	0	0
	1	1	1
Even Parity Bit	0	1	1
Odd Parity Bit	1	0	0

The letter S comprises four 1's in total. For even parity, a 1 is added if necessary to make the number of 1's an even amount. Otherwise, a 0 is added. So, for even parity a 0 is added in this case. For odd parity, however, a 1 would be added to make the total number of 1's up to an odd number.

In the case of no parity, nothing is added.

The parity bit is sent along with the data to the receiving computer. The receiving computer will then calculate its own parity bit and compare it with that which has been sent. If the two are alike, all is well. If not, some problem has arisen.

Once again the programs the computers are running must be set up in the same way, i.e., both even parity, both odd parity, or both no parity.

Transmission Speed

The rate of transmission between two computers must be decided before the transmission takes place. It is measured in bits per second (bps) or *Baud*. One Baud is roughly the same as 1 bps. Normal transmission speeds are:

         300 bps
         600
       1 200
       2 400
       4 800
       9 600
      19 200

The higher the bps, the quicker the data transfer and the lower the telephone costs.

300 bps is not very quick. To send or receive a 90 kbyte file would take about an hour. The same file would take around 10–15 minutes at 1200 bps or only a few minutes at 9600 bps.

The highest speed you can use is determined by your modem and that of the connected computer. You can't send at 2400 bps if the receiving modem can only manage 1200 bps.

Simplex and Duplex

A telephone line can be used in three different ways: *simplex*, *half duplex*, or *full duplex*.

Simplex means that data transfer can only be done in one direction. Videotext services that send stock market quotes over your TV set are an example of this.

Half duplex means that data can be sent both ways, but only one direction at a time.

Full duplex means that data can be sent both ways and in both directions at the same time, just like when you talk on the phone.

Null-modems

It is also possible to connect two computers without using a modem. You will still need to run a communications program on both computers. You will also need to connect the two computers with a special null-modem or straight through serial cable instead of the usual modem cable.

Viruses – Am I At Risk?

A *data virus* is an "electronic disease" that can be deliberately introduced into your computer. Basically, they are small programs that will destroy information on your hard disk (often at a date) or display unwanted messages on your screen.

As long as you work with your own computer and don't communicate with others you're not likely to be hit by one of these things. However, as soon as you start communicating with a bulletin board system (BBS) there is a small chance that your computer may pick up a data virus that is transmitted along with another file you receive. However, the system operators usually know about most viruses and keep their bulletin boards "clean," thus minimizing the risks.

Data viruses can also be passed on via a floppy disk! For example, your friend might have received a program and unknowingly a virus as well, then if he makes a copy for you on a diskette, the virus can be introduced into your system as well.

A user will not generally know when his or her computer has picked up a virus until something drastic happens, like the hard disk getting reformatted.

Anti-virus programs are available. They will help you find any virus that comes along.

Checklist

For successful data communications you need:

- A computer with a serial port.
- A modem attached to the serial port.
- A telephone line.
- A communications program.
- The right settings for the communications program, i.e., transmission speed, parity, number of data bits and stop bits, etc. Check your communications program's handbook for further details.

Living With a Computer

Chapter 9   If you're only going to be using your PC in a company in which most of the staff already use PCs, then you don't need to read this chapter. For in such an office, you probably already have a desk that can house the keyboard, CPU, and monitor, a stand to hold your printer and the paper it will consume, a device that can protect your computer against power surges, and sufficient storage space for computer manuals and diskettes.

But what if you're installing your computer at home? Or, what if you work for a small company that's never tried to accommodate staff using PCs regularly? In these cases, this chapter can be one of the most valuable in the entire book.

Where Do I Put My Computer?

A problem faced by nearly everyone the first time they buy a computer is where to keep it. Unfortunately, most furniture designed prior to the computer age does very poorly when it comes to providing space for a computer and all its accessories. In the case of an IBM-PC, the problem is actually a bit worse as there are actually three components to worry about: the CPU, the keyboard, and the monitor.

The main problem involves the keyboard. For, while a detached keyboard is universally recommended by office design experts as the most comfortable and versatile type of design, the combined depth of the CPU and the keyboard unit is about 24 inches, which is about 6 inches more than the depth of a standard typing extension (or typing carry) that's attached to most office desks. You can't just put the computer and the keyboard on your desk, because the desk is too high. Specifically, the PC keyboard should be used on a surface which is about 26 inches off the floor – which is the height of a typing carry and computer desk – rather than on standard desk tops which are typically 29 inches off the floor. While the extra 3 inches may not seem like a lot as you read this, your arms, wrists, and fingers will tell you this is a MASSIVE difference the first time you try typing 20 or 30 pages on a standard desk.

For extended home use, the best solution is to buy a computer desk and perhaps a matching printer stand as well. Computer desks needn't be expensive. Companies such as O'Sullivan and Bush specialize in selling attractive well-designed desks that start at as little as $100. For about $350, you can get a unit that will look right at home in any well furnished home office.

A very common and efficient arrangement is to buy a desk that comes with a matching hutch with adjustable shelves. In this case, you usually put the keyboard in front of where you'll sit. Put the monitor on a shelf in the hutch with the shelf at a height so the monitor is just about at eye level. Then you can either put the CPU at the back of the desk, under the hutch so that it's as much out of the way as possible; or you can put it on the floor, so that it stands vertically with the disk drive slots at the top. Use the remaining shelves in the hutch to hold your program manuals, diskettes, etc.

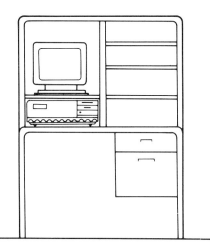

A variation of this approach is to buy a computer desk and a metal, jointed arm that clamps to the desk. With this kind of arrangement the keyboard once again goes in front of you. The monitor goes on the movable platform attached to the arm. The CPU goes on the floor, at the back of the desk, or under the monitor on the platform.

While these are probably the two best approaches, they both require you to buy a computer desk. If you just don't want to do this you can also buy a sliding metal tray that bolts to the undersurface of your present desk or work table to hold your keyboard. The CPU can go on the floor, on the desk, or on a moveable platform. The monitor can then go on the desk so that it's on top of the CPU, on a moveable platform, or on a shelf of the hutch.

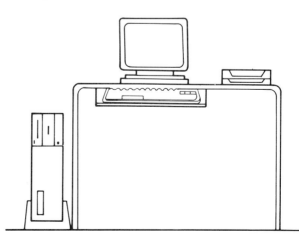

A word of warning about computer desks: they usually come as "knockdown" units that attractive models at computer shows are able to assemble in less than 15 minutes. However, if you are not an attractive model or an engineer, plan to spend at least two hours putting the darn thing together.

While you're at it, whether you improvise around your present office furniture or buy a computer desk, consider buying a printer stand. Selling for between $75 and $150 for a "knockdown" unit, they are nearly indispensable if you own or plan to buy a laser or wide carriage printer. The better designed printer stands have two or three shelves to hold paper stock of different sizes, so that any size can be easily routed to the printer; and they have a basket attached to the back of the stand to hold the printer output. If you do decide to buy one of the knockdown desks, a matching printer stand is almost always available.

Two Final Points About Situating Your PC

First, since the reset button on many CPUs is on the back, and you will need to get to this control every so often, try to place the CPU so that you can reach the reset button easily from a sitting position. This argues against placing the CPU on a back corner of your desk (as is sometimes suggested in office furniture catalogs) if your reset button is indeed on the back of the CPU.

Also, try to arrange things so that the monitor is at eye level, and is directly in front of you, about 12 to 18 inches away. For long stretches at the keyboard, this is much better than arrangements which require you to turn your head to the side, tilt your head upwards, or squint because the monitor's so far away.

Protecting Your Investment

One of the cheapest forms of insurance available for the PC is a good *surge protector*. This will protect your computer when voltage spikes occur. Without one of these "AC clamping devices" (as techies call them), you are always running the risk of having aberrations in the local power lines damage your computer or disks.

The better devices of this type include from three to six sockets so that accessories can be protected as well; and an EMI-RFI filtering circuit which prevents electronic emissions from the PC and devices such as the printer from interfering with nearby televisions, videotape recorders, and audio systems. The latter feature is particularly useful with the less expensive PC clones since some of these give off enough emissions to really annoy your neighbors or co-workers.

If you use a modem with your computer, consider buying an EMI-RFI filter that can also protect you against power surges entering your computer through your phone line. While this is not a common occurrence, it can happen and the units that include this feature aren't much more expensive than those that don't have it.

If you frequently work on documents that are very difficult to replicate, you might consider buying an *uninterruptable power supply* (called a UPS) in place of an ordinary surge protector. This is really nothing more than a huge rechargeable battery – much like the one in your car – that's placed between the electric circuit in your wall and your PC.

With one of these devices, electricity flows from the wall, into the UPS, and then into your computer. Because the electricity in the UPS is first converted from AC current to DC current, and then back from DC current to AC current, your computer is totally "*isolated*" (another techie term) from your household current. Thus, even if your house is struck by lightening – something that will fry most surge protectors in an instant – no damage can come to your computer.

Even more importantly, if you should have a "brownout" that reduces your flow of electricity, or a "blackout" that causes you to lose electricity altogether, the UPS kicks in within a fraction of a second. This means that instead of losing the document you're working on and risking a "*head crash*" in which your computer's hard disk drive is ruined, an alarm will go off which means that you have from 5–10 minutes to complete what you're working on, save your files, and turn the computer off. In the meantime, your computer just chugs right along, powered by the UPS battery, completely oblivious to the fact that it's no longer receiving power from the wall.

UPS devices aren't cheap; they typically cost from $300 to $600 each. But if you value your time, live where blackouts and brownouts are rife, and want to avoid damage to your equipment, they're well worth the cost.

Protecting Your Files and Programs

Another area of concern is disk storage. It doesn't take long to accumulate a fairly large collection of floppy disks containing both programs and data. Storage soon becomes an important issue.

For maximum protection, disks should be stored in a nonmetallic dust-free environment. Many stores sell plastic file boxes which store from 50 to 75 disks and come with a dust cover. While some of these also come with $20 to $40 price tags, equally good ones can often be found for less than $10.

For reasons of convenience, most PC owners keep their working copies of disks near their computers. However, experienced users also keep a second storage box in a different location in their workrooms for backup copies of data and programs. This location should not be within arm's reach of the computer. This minimizes the possibility of getting present copies and backup copies of disks confused with one another. And, as we will discuss later on, you should always make backup copies. Nothing is more discouraging than to spend several hours working on a computer, and then to lose all of one's work in one moment of carelessness.

Is Your PC Insured?

Consider getting a special insurance policy to cover your computer and your purchased software. Without a special rider that insures computers used for business purposes, many homeowners policies won't cover any equipment used for business purposes. Also, even if you do have such a rider, it may not cover damage to disks or equipment caused by carelessness or accident.

Because of these problems, be sure you check your homeowners policy to see what is and what is not covered, and check to see if a special rider is available. If it is, the $50-$100 extra you'll pay for it is well worth the cost.

If a rider isn't available, or if it's too restrictive or expensive, a special computer policy offering "all-risk" coverage is often a good idea. A typical policy providing all-risk coverage with only a $50 deductible sells for about $100 for $10,000 of coverage.

Communicating With the Outside World

The room where you do most of your computer work should be equipped with a telephone and a modular telephone jack. Ideally, the telephone should be within an arm's reach of the keyboard. This is useful when you are calling a software company or a friend for help with a problem. With a telephone within arm's reach, you can actually do the suggested operations while you are on the phone. Also, sooner or later you will add a modem to your system so that you can communicate with other computers, and in this case the telephone and telephone jack will be essential.

As PC owners become more involved with communications, the next step is to add a dedicated telephone line in the computer room. This permits the modem to be permanently connected to one line which will then be used almost exclusively for data communications while the original line is again used exclusively for voice communications. With this kind of set-up, one can be talking to an associate on the voice line while programs are flowing back and forth on the data line. Also, with the proper modem and software, this system permits a PC to automatically answer calls on the communications line and to send or receive data without anyone being present. This capability permits one to run one's own bulletin board; or to arrange for data transfer in and out of an office on the weekends and during evening hours.

Still another reason for adding communications capability to your computer room is to permit you to add a fax board to your computer, or to use a separate fax machine. No, this won't mean adding a THIRD phone line. For all but the most rapid communications junkies, the fax machine or fax board can coexist quite nicely on the same phone line that serves the modem. However, it's also overkill to expect voice, modem and fax communications to coexist peacefully on only one phone line; so if you're going to have all three kinds of communications, put in at least two phone lines.

The Smart Buyer's Guide to Acquiring Hardware and Software

Chapter 10   Today's PC marketplace is both good and bad for novice buyers. It's good from the standpoint that it's getting increasingly difficult to buy either hardware or software that's unreliable or of poor quality. It's bad from the perspective that with so many products and sources to choose from, coming up with the "best buy" is often an exercise in frustration.

In this chapter we'll deal first with the question of from whom should you buy hardware and software, and then we'll go on to give you a detailed example of how you should go about making a substantial purchase.

From Whom Should I Buy?

There are five major sources of computer software and hardware from which you can buy. For lack of a better way to classify them, we'll give these sources the following names:

Full-price stores
Discount stores
Mail order firms
Consultants & VARs
Manufacturers who sell by mail

The first thing to realize about this list is that these categories are far from being clear-cut; and secondly, realize that it's very hard to generalize about these sources since each of them has ample numbers of both heroes and villains. In the sections below, we'll try to help you decide which sources are right for you.

Full-price Stores

If you go into a store that sells software and hardware for close to list price, you've got an absolute right to expect knowledgeable salespeople who will spend lots of time with you. They should give you hands-on demonstrations of the products in which you're interested; and should also give you some after-sales support such as doing simple hardware installations and allowing you to attend classes given at the store at no extra cost.

They also should be ready to give you basic support on most of the products they sell. Thus if your new computer fails in the first few weeks, they should be willing to swap it out for a loaner or an entirely new unit; and if you can't figure out how to save your *WordPerfect* document, you should be able to call them on the telephone and learn how to do it.

These retailers can provide most of these services because, if you do pay close to list price, they're enjoying a 30–50 percent markup on most of the merchandise they're selling. Sure, these are the dealers who are likely to be in the high rent locations, but with the difference between what these dealers charge and what discount dealers will settle for, you DESERVE these kinds of support.

However, you can't be greedy. Unless you've bought a special service policy or there's a very generous manufacturer's warranty, even full-price dealers can't afford to swap out your system eight months after you've bought it. Similarly, they can't either afford be expected to answer all of your software questions. At some point you'll have to start dealing with the software manufacturer.

If you want a rule-of-thumb as to how much support you "deserve," compute the difference between what you've paid and what the lowest published mail order prices are for the same products, and then take half that amount. To our minds, the number you'll end up with is a good indicator of how much the full price dealer can afford to spend on you in terms of special services.

Thus, if you've just paid $3995 for a Super AT clone that's been delivered to you with a surge protector, this book, and 3 software packages, and the best mail order prices you can find for the same items total $3295, you can assume that you're entitled to ($3995 – $3295)/2 = $350 worth of special services.

But please understand, in today's market $350 worth of services doesn't go as far as you might think. For instance, a service technicians' time is worth $50 an hour, a software expert's time usually goes for about the same amount, and the cost of attending a full-day class is around $300.

Thus if you got a half-day course in DOS, the store's 12-month "fix or exchange in 48 hours" warranty, and free installation of the machine in your office included in that $3995 price, congratulate yourself! You've just gotten a tremendous bargain!

Discount Stores

When people envision a discount computer store, they usually picture it as being a store in a seedy part of town with unopened boxes piled all over the floor. And while there are many discount operations that look like this, there are also many that arc attractive and located in malls and prime locations.

It's also hard to generalize about the service offered by discount stores. The stores of some of the large discount chains, for instance, are the ONLY places that will let you return any software package after you've opened and used it for a month. Other stores CAN'T do this; their volume doesn't give them the clout to force distributors to sell to them on those terms.

Some of the best service is sometimes obtained from single-owner discount stores who've realized that they need to provide superb service if they're to grow and prosper. If the owner of a small store is a techie who buys computer components and builds clones from them in the back of the store, he might well be willing to provide you with the same "fix or exchange in 48 hours" warranty on his Peoria Smasher 1000 System since he's got confidence in his own work and knows he can replace any of its components in 20 minutes flat.

There are also lots of discount stores that provide only the manufacturers' warranties, and don't want to take the time to explain the features of their products to you.

Should you buy from these stores? If you're reading this book for any reason other than academic interest – probably not! But two years from now, when you're comfortable using PCs and know what hardware and software you need, you might well want to patronize these dealers. They frequently offer a combination of rock-bottom prices and instant availability that's hard to beat.

Mail Order Dealers

Ask any experienced PC buyer and they'll tell you that the mail order firms are the "market makers" for both hardware and software. In other words, their prices and policies are used as the baseline against which other sources are compared.

The best of the mail order dealers offer some services that other sources have trouble matching. For instance, many of them offer unconditional 30-day refund privileges on hardware, as well as software purchases. Some offer terrific telephone support, such as letting you make a free phone call to one of their technicians who will happily spend 45 minutes talking you through the procedure by which you can install the hard disk you've just purchased from them in your computer. And some offer 90-day in-office (or in-home) service contracts with a well known national repair firm at no extra cost.

They can do these things because of the unique way they do business. For instance, because they sell so many hard disks, they can afford to train a relatively low-paid technician so that he or she knows everything there is to know about installing them in machines at home. Similarly, they can offer 90-day in-office repair contracts because the national repair firms behind them use these free 90-day contracts as a way of selling you long-term contracts.

But all isn't rosy in buying from mail order dealers. There have been several well publicized incidents in the past few years regarding mail order firms that cashed customers checks but then didn't fill the orders.

Also, as with the discount stores, there are many mail order stores that offer no services beyond having very low prices. There are also mail order catalog firms that actually charge list price for their products and don't offer much in the way of services. However, since they do sometimes offer products that are hard to find, even these firms aren't necessarily bad to buy from.

The best rules in buying from mail order firms are:

1) buy only by credit card;

2) try to buy from stores whose ads have been running for at least a year; and

3) don't assume that mail order prices are the lowest you'll find.

The reason you should buy only by credit card is that, regardless of what the store says, if merchandise isn't delivered, or is defective or misrepresented, you can contact the credit card company and they'll usually provide you with full credit if you've received the item within the last 30 days. The merchant really has no say in this, since all the credit card company does is deduct the refund from monies due to the store. As far as the credit card companies are concerned, the store is guilty until proven innocent. Thus, as long as the store is still in business, if you buy by credit card you've got excellent protection against fraud.

You should try to buy from mail order firms whose ads have been running for at least a year because that's a good indication that the company is alive and well. Of course, this rule can't always be used with stores that advertise by direct mail, but it's useful for those that advertise in magazines.

And again, don't assume that mail order prices are the lowest you'll find. Compare prices and take into account the services you will or will not receive. Novice users might want to wait until they've got some experience before they start making major purchases by mail since there's really no substitute for the hands-on assistance and encouragement a high quality store can offer.

Consultants and VARs

Consultants and VARs are still another source of hardware and software. VARs are "*Value-Added Retailers*." This is fancy way of saying that they're firms that can sell you equipment but that don't have store fronts. Like consultants, they typically work out of office buildings or their homes, and they'll usually come to you rather than having you come to them.

Consultants and VARs like to say that they sell SOLUTIONS, not hardware and software. They see their role as:

- helping you determine your computing needs;
- going out and buying the hardware and software that's necessary to meet those needs;
- customizing the software until it does exactly what you need it to do;
- offering the training and support that's needed to keep everything operating in your office.

Is there a difference between a consultant and a VAR? Not really, so from now on we'll speak just of VARs.

The first thing you've got to realize is that VARs can be one of the least expensive or most expensive sources of hardware and software. It all depends on how they structure their businesses.

Some VARs like to sell their time. For prices that now average $100-$150 an hour, they'll do all the things described above. And, if you're willing to pay those rates, they'll frequently pass onto you nearly the full discount they receive from distributors and manufacturers, thus allowing you to purchase items at close to their actual cost.

Other VARs see themselves as being dealers without stores. These do the "system work" for free or at minimal cost, but charge close to the full list price for the hardware and software they sell you.

There are other VARs that offer you the WORST of both worlds. Typically this happens when professionals in other fields try to function as VARs. Thus, if an accountant tries to sell you software at its full list price and charge rates to his full hourly rate to install it, beware! You shouldn't have to pay the full freight on both ends of the deal.

If you're a complete novice when it comes to using computers, or if you have very specialized needs that personnel in most stores can't deal with, dealing with a VAR can make a lot of sense. The right ones already know your business, and within an hour of meeting you they can identify 90 percent of the hardware and software you need! This can save you a small fortune, as anyone who has ever bought the WRONG hardware and software can attest.

Further, a VAR may well have already written modules of computer code for other clients that he or she can use for your application as well. This can save you thousands of dollars and months of frustration, when compared to you having to customize store-bought software yourself.

This brings up an important point: No matter from whom you buy software, realize that much of it requires customizing before it can be used in your business. Thus, you can't just buy *Lotus 1-2-3* and start to do cash flow analyses. First, someone has to enter your data into the computer, then someone has to write a program that will generate the analyses.

It's these kinds of things – along with selecting the right hardware and software – that VARs do best. And if your firm's own resources don't include people with these skills, don't hesitate to look towards a good VAR.

To deal effectively with a VAR, get a clear agreement between you as to the basis upon which you'll be charged and what the VAR will and will not do. Also, try to structure the job in stages which permit you to bail out along the way.

You might want to start by negotiating a small fixed price contract with the VAR to do an analysis of your needs. He or she should present you with an overall design, specify the commercial hardware and software you'll need initially, give you the best prices and sources, and give you an overall cost estimate for building the system you need in stages that you can probably afford.

In effect, by doing this, you'll be paying the VAR to write you a detailed proposal. Because this is largely a marketing activity, you should pay much less than the VAR's usual rate for such a report. Experienced VARs typically charge from $500 to $5000 to do this for most small business applications; while other VARs – the ones who want to make their money on the equipment sales – will offer to do the job for "free." The latter is the classic IBM approach to marketing and you can be sure that one way or another you'll end up paying for what you get.

If what you get looks good and you enjoy working together, then you can go on to other activities in which the system you need is built and installed in stages. Try to structure things so that first, you get up and running with a very basic system that doesn't have all the bells and whistles you'll eventually want; then add the enhancements in later stages when you have a much better idea of what you actually need.

Manufacturers Who Sell By Mail

Many respected hardware and software companies sell directly by mail to users such as yourself. It costs close to a million dollars to pay for the ads, packaging, and promotion needed to create the "pull" that dealers demand before they'll actually put PC products on their shelves. This causes many manufacturers to sell by mail instead.

Among the better companies, customer support is often unexcelled since there's no one standing between you and the developer; and typically the programmer or engineer who gives you support has played a major role in developing or refining the product. Also, because most manufacturers have very limited product lines and an emotional investment in what they're selling, they're truly interested in helping you succeed with their product and will do everything possible to help you.

To protect yourself when ordering from manufacturers, try to pay by credit card. Also, if you're ordering a product you're not familiar with, ask them to send you some product reviews of either the product in which you're interested or earlier versions of it. With literally hundreds of magazines and newspapers publishing product reviews, you might want to be especially cautious if the manufacturer can't supply you with some of them. If you've got a fax, just ask to have the reviews faxed to you and you'll have them in minutes.

Don't assume that just because you're buying from the manufacturer you're getting the best price. If a manufacturer is trying to sell simultaneously by mail and through dealers, he may charge full list price in his mail solicitations so as not to discourage distributors and dealers from handling the product.

How To Select Computer Products

The average "*half-life*" of a software product in the United States is now about nine months. This means that half of all the PC software programs introduced this month will either be updated or pulled off the market within the next four-and-a-half months.

Prices are equally volatile. The prices of basic components such as memory chips can either halve or double within 30–60 days, and this causes the prices of the devices that use those components to fluctuate wildly at times.

Then there are compatibility problems. Imagine the chaos if Ford cars couldn't use Exxon gasoline, GM cars demanded it, and Toyotas could only tolerate it if you added a special accessory filter. Yet this is exactly the situation you face when adding hardware or software to a computer system.

Let's take a look at monitors, for instance. There are now at least four different kinds of monitors, each of which demand that a different kind of graphics card be installed in the computer. But even if the right card is installed, some monitors can only be used by programs that have special "drivers" designed to be used with it. And, even if you have the right kind of graphics card, it may not work with your computer!

Get the idea? The PC industry is far from the point where any computer can use "any kind of gas."

So what does this mean to you? Given all of these problems, how do you get a reasonably good buy? The answer is: *Do your homework and check with several sources before you buy anything.* Here is an example of how you might want to proceed.

What A Smart Buyer Does

Let's assume that you've got a fairly basic beginners' system that you bought a few years ago. It's an IBM-PC with 2 floppy disk drives, 640K of memory, a CGA color monitor, and a dot matrix printer.

Now you've decided that you're tired of paying $500 a shot to have a typesetting service pasteup and generate the type for your company's newsletter that you distribute every 2 weeks. You figure that by adding a desktop publishing system to your existing IBM-PC, or even by buying a second PC that can do desktop publishing, you'll be able to pay for the new hardware and software out of the $13,000 you're paying annually for typesetting. But because you're still going to have to pay for the labor, you decide that all you can afford to spend is $5000.

Well, how do you start? Probably the best way to start is by first deciding what kind of software you'll need to produce the kind of newsletter you have in mind. To do this, talk to friends and business acquaintances who are already producing newsletters themselves, visit some software dealers to see what they recommend, and look at every magazine article you can find on the subject.

As a result of these activities, you decide that the desktop publishing package called *Ventura Publisher* is the package that you need. Do you just go out and buy *Ventura Publisher*? Not on your life! First you've got to find out if it will run on your existing system. If you check the documentation that comes with the package, you will find that it requires at least an AT-type computer with a hard disk, and that a laser printer and high resolution monitor are "strongly recommended."

In computer lingo "strongly recommended" means: "We DARE you to ignore our advice." So what you've learned so far is that you're going to need an entirely new computer system, since literally none of your existing components can be used with *Ventura Publisher*.

Should this discourage you? Of course not! Since you've gone this far, why not go a bit further and see what this new toy will cost you. To do this, summarize your needs in a single coherent paragraph that you can transfer to an index card that can be carried around in your pocket. It might read:

"I want an AT-type computer system that I can use primarily to typeset a newsletter using *Ventura Publisher*. According to the *Ventura* manual and what I've read, I need at least a 40-megabyte hard disk, an inexpensive high-resolution monitor, and a laser printer. I want to keep the total cost under $5000, including everything. What equipment do you recommend that I purchase and how much will it cost?"

You might start by buying copies of all the magazines you can find that are featuring desktop publishing in the current issue, and then calling one or two of the large mail order firms that advertise them for product recommendations and quotes. You will probably get an answer like this one: "We can sell you an AT-clone and a 40-meg disk for only $1400. *Ventura* will cost you $450. And we've got a "clone" of the Hewlett-Packard laser printer for $1700. But you'll have to go elsewhere for the high resolution monochrome monitor, as we don't sell one."

This brings the mail order cost for the system to about $3550, plus the cost of the monitor for which you've yet to get a price. Now is the time to visit a few stores. Why wait until now? Because you already have some idea of what you need and the minimum it's likely to cost.

After visiting a few stores, you find that the monitors you want range from about $750 to $1500. After looking at their screens, you decide that you can easily live with the $750 unit. You've also learned that the store prices for the equipment and software for which you've received mail order quotes is about $4200, but that includes a genuine Laserjet II, not a clone.

So now you've got two viable choices:

You can order everything but the monitor by mail for $3550, spend $750 for the monitor at a local store, and have your daughter's hacker boyfriend Leroy, help you connect everything and install the software. This is the $4300 rock bottom price alternative.

Or:

You can buy everything at your local store for $4950, where they'll also throw in free installation and a 1-day "Introduction to *Ventura Publisher*" seminar.

Either of these choices is workable. Even if you don't have some-one to help you install the hardware and software, you can probably do the job yourself; especially if you're willing to invest in a few phone calls to the help-lines maintained by the mail order firm and *Ventura Publisher*. And you'll probably find that the superb tutorial that comes with *Ventura* will give you much more information than will be imparted in the seminar. Still, the store's price is more than fair, considering what they're offering.

If You Don't Have the Time

And what if you don't have the time to do all this? Well that's why consultants and VARs exist. For an application as "simple" as this, a VAR that specializes in desktop publishing would be able to sit down with you, take a look at some recent issues of your newsletter and your present equipment, and tell you on-the-spot what equipment you need. Then, after making an assessment of what you will need to learn before you can operate on your own, they'll probably go away and return the next day with a package price that includes the equipment, installation, and customized hands-on training at your place of work.

The cost for all of this is likely to be in the $5000-$7500 range, depending upon how much you already know about matters ranging from graphic design to using your computer system. If you get the low figure, $5000, it means that the VAR is confident that they can install your equipment and get you started using it in less than a day. The equipment will probably cost them about $3500, and they're charging you $1500 for their knowledge and a day of installation and training. They're looking for about a 20 % profit margin. At the high end, $7500, they're planning to give you 4 days of training and support; and they're looking for a 25 % profit.

Don't forget, in specifying the equipment you need and doing the shopping for you, they're doing more than "just" saving you 2–3 days of shopping. More important, they are guaranteeing the compatibility of the entire system and the quality of the components. This has considerable worth in a complex area such as desktop publishing; especially if they'll back it up with their own "48-hour fix or replace" guarantee.

Thus, you can see that you've got lots of alternatives when it comes to buying hardware and software; and none of them are clearly superior. Rather, how you buy and from whom you buy depends upon how much you already know and how much time you're willing to invest.

An OS/2 Briefing

Chapter 11   Newcomers to the world of the PC and its compatibles are often confronted with terms and ideas that are so alien that many are scared off by them. Incessant talk about a new operating system called OS/2 has most newcomers scared to death. Typically new users ask, "Do I need OS/2 and should I buy it now?" The fact is, OS/2 is the operating system of the future for the PC, but the future is a few years away.

For now, all the new user needs to do is understand a few things about OS/2 to know all he or she needs to know.

a) OS/2 requires gobs of memory – at least 2 megabytes to do anything, with 8–16 megabytes recommended.

b) There are few applications available running under the OS/2 operating system.

c) OS/2 completely replaces DOS, but DOS can be run as a so-called task within the OS/2 operating system. But OS/2 cannot operate under DOS.

d) OS/2 can be run without a shell program called the presentation manager – dubbed PM by the writers. When the user does this, the operating system looks nearly identical to DOS and uses most of the same commands.

e) It's expensive.

What OS/2 is designed to do is improve the overall performance and usability of the machines. Right now a DOS machine can only do one task at a time without special software patches that many times hurt the machine's performance and sometimes tend to crash the system. DOS wasn't built for more than one task at a time. OS/2 is designed with multi-tasking in mind.

Also, OS/2 is designed to get away from the DOS prompt interface (C:>) and head towards the most popular interface fad, called the *GUI* or *Graphical User Interface*. This means that the display will be boxed, colorful with icons and symbols, and require a new way of doing things. Instead of typing in commands, you use a pointing device such as a mouse to move an arrow on the screen and have it point at a particular application name or icon (a small drawing symbolically depicting the application). You click on the mouse button twice (fast) and the program loads. This can be very fast and efficient once one gets used to it. The idea was popularized by the Macintosh and you should play with that machine before even considering such an interface on a PC. The mouse is also used to drag items (as though they were objects) around the screen for repositioning or for convenience.

The OS/2 GUI interface also introduces to the user a concept called *windowing*. You can create ersatz windows or openings on the screen into which a program may be placed and executed. In other "windows," other programs, different ones, can be set to run. In fact the screen can be full of windows, each showing a different program.

The programs which currently are designed for and work well with OS/2 include special OS/2 versions of *Paradox*, *WordPerfect*, *Lotus 1-2-3*, and *Logicomm*. More are being released every day. IBM recently showed a huge line-up of interesting applications all designed for OS/2.

When people talk about OS/2 they talk about improved design ideas that are not perceived by every user as important, but they are. For example, OS/2 has what is called a *High Performance File System* (HPFS) which breaks away from the old-fashioned *File Allocation Table* (FAT) technology used by DOS and by the first version of OS/2. The FAT technique is a slow way to read and write files to and from a disk. The HPFS technology speeds up read-write performance dramatically. This will pay off in improved overall system performance which is what OS/2 is all about.

It's one of many advanced ideas used in the design of OS/2. Still, we all wonder when will we really have to switch to OS/2.

The president of Compaq Computers, Rod Canion, summed it up in a recent interview when he said, "The biggest problem that OS/2 has had is the unreal expectations that people have placed on it. In our mind it's very clearly the next generation beyond DOS. DOS has evolved, and will continue to evolve, as a single user, single-tasking kind of operating system. Future applications will require multi-tasking capability. OS/2 is the evolution of DOS into that arena. People will eventually need OS/2, and they won't move to OS/2 because they like OS/2. People will be pulled toward OS/2 by applications that justify the cost and the change of operating system."

And one must evaluate the price for sure. OS/2 is an expensive addition to the computer system. The price for the basic kernel of OS/2 (standard edition) is $325. Add optional capabilities and the price skyrockets. The applications running under OS/2 aren't cheap either. Most start at $500 and work their way up. Worse, there is no shareware or inexpensive entry level software for OS/2.

PC Week summed up one attitude about OS/2 that needs repeating, "After reviewing all the promises and problems of OS/2, you may decide it's better to forget this new operating system entirely. Most of your employees or customers may be perfectly happy with running single-tasking DOS applications. To make this decision, you'll need to weigh the cost of upgrading your equipment from DOS to OS/2 and the expected business benefits to be gained from OS/2."

The expense of OS/2 is the key to deciding on whether you want to explore its use. For OS/2 you need:

- 2 to 16 megabytes of main memory
- a fast 80286 or 80386-based computer
- a roomy and fast hard disk with at least 80 megabytes of storage
- a mouse
- all new software

and

- an expensive VGA monitor and video display card are recommended.

So you can see why OS/2 has not taken off like a rocket. For right now, it's likely further improvements in DOS will keep most of the PC world happy and OS/2 will evolve for specialized tasks. Eventually the two worlds will join.

Appendices

A. Using the Optional Diskette

In this appendix, you will find instructions on how to install the programs supplied on the optional diskette, which we call the MASTER disk.

The installation process is described in three different sections. You should follow the section that applies to your computer system:

- Installation on a two disk drive system
- Installation on a one disk drive system
- Installation on a hard disk system

Installation on a Two Disk Drive System

You are going to create a copy of your MASTER disk so that you don't have to use it, and risk damaging it.

- Start your computer and wait for the A: > system prompt.
- Remove SYSTEM disk used to start the computer from drive A.
- Insert the MASTER disk in drive A.
- Insert a formatted disk in drive B.
- Type the following:

  ```
  copy a:*.* b:
  ```

- Press the ⏎ key.

Installation On a One Disk Drive System

You are going to create a copy of your MASTER disk so that you don't have to use it, and risk damaging it. As you only have one disk drive, copying will involve swapping disks several times.

- Start your computer and wait for the A: > system prompt.
- Remove SYSTEM disk used to start the computer.
- Insert the MASTER disk in the drive.
- Type the following (including spaces after copy and after *.*):

  copy a:*.* b:

- Press the ↵ key.

Because of the large amount of information to be copied, you may have to change disks several times.

When the following message (or a similar one) is displayed on your screen, you should place the MASTER disk in the drive unit and then press the ↵ key:

```
Insert disk for drive A and strike
any key when ready
```

When the following message (or a similar one) is displayed on your screen, you should place the formatted disk in the drive unit and press the ↵ key:

```
Insert disk for drive B and strike
any key when ready
```

- Insert a formatted disk in drive B when required.
- Insert the MASTER disk in drive A when required.

Installation On a Hard Disk System

- Start your computer and wait for the C: \> system prompt.

The first step is to create a directory for the programs. You may wish to call the directory **pcsurv**.

- Type the following:

```
md \pcsurv
```

- Press the ↵ key.

Next, copy all the files from the MASTER disk to the newly created directory.

- Put the MASTER disk in drive A.
- Type the following (including spaces after copy and after *.*):

```
copy a:*.* c:\pcsurv
```

- Press the ↵ key.

To use the programs on your hard drive, you first have to change directories into the **pcsurv** directory.

Type the following:

```
cd \pcsurv
```

Using the Programs

To use all but one of the programs, simply type:

PCCR

This calls up a menu that offers you the use of:

- the 150-lesson keyboard trainer
- the communications simulator
- your private mastery test

The menu also allows you to:

- get more information by pressing the **Help** key, **F1**
- adjust the colors on your screen by pressing **F2**
- leave the program by pressing the **Exit** key, **F10**

As you use the different programs controlled by this menu, you'll find that pressing **F1** will always allow you to get more information. Get in the habit of pressing **F1** whenever you come to a screen for the first time. In Typing Tutor, **F1** gives you the proper finger placements for the different keys.

Pressing **F10** will allow you to leave the activity you're working on. Continually pressing **F10** will cause you to exit from the menu system.

The diskette also contains a terrific directory program called **ID.EXE** which is written by John Gaines who manages our Help Line. It's a very powerful variant of the DIR program supplied with DOS that's also a lot easier to use. When you're about to type DIR, type ID instead. Full documentation is provided in a filed called **ID302.DOC** that you can either read or print using your word processor.

Finally, the diskette also contains some small text files that are used along with the exercises in the book.

We hope you'll enjoy using this diskette. Both the typing tutor and the directory program are worth more than you paid for the book and the diskette!

IF YOU HAVE ANY PROBLEMS, PLEASE CALL OUR HELP LINE

301-294-7453 MON–FRI 9–5 (est)

B. Some Useful DOS Commands

This appendix summarizes some of the most useful DOS commands. Most of these have been covered in this book, but a few "extras" are included to help you widen your knowledge of DOS.

Remember that internal commands are readily available from your computer's memory, while external commands require the actual DOS program. This means that disk users will have to insert their DOS disk in the relevant drive to be able to use the command. External commands are marked with an asterisk (*) in the following table.

The following commands are described:

BACKUP	Make backup copy of hard disk content*
RESTORE	Restore (recopy) files to hard disk*
CD	Change subdirectory
CHKDSK	Check disk*
CLS	Clear screen
COPY	Copy files
DATE	Change the computer's date
DEL	Delete files
DIR	Display list of filenames
DISKCOMP	Compare disks
DISKCOPY	Copy disk
FORMAT	Format disk
MD	Create (make) subdirectory
PROMPT	Change prompt
RD	Remove (delete) subdirectory
TIME	Change the computer's time
TYPE	Type the contents of a file

Note:
The examples given in this appendix are just that: examples. You may well have to adapt the commands to suit your own needs.

Make Backup Copy of Hard Disk Content (BACKUP)

This command can be used to make backup copies of all or some of the files on your hard disk. The backup copies are made on disks. You can even copy files that would not normally fit onto a single disk (customer files for example). These big files are divided automatically onto a number of disks.

One disadvantage of this command is that the files on the disks cannot be used in the normal way. Instead, they must first be restored (recopied) back into the same subdirectory on the hard disk using the RESTORE command. Moreover, you can encounter problems when you try to restore (using RESTORE) program files that are write-protected. As a result, you should only copy unprotected program files and data files. This command is on your DOS disk (and normally on your hard disk as well).

Before you start, you must have a number of formatted disks available (see section on the FORMAT command in this Appendix). The number you will need depends on how much you wish to copy. You should number the disks starting with 1, and they must be in the proper sequence when you restore the files to the hard disk.

- Insert the first formatted disk in drive A and type one of the following:

`backup c:*.* a:`	This copies all files in the subdirectory in question onto drive A.
`backup c:*.* a:/s`	This copies all files on the hard disk that are in the subdirectory in question and also all files in all lower subdirectories onto drive A.
`backup c:*.* a:/m`	This searches through all of the files on the hard disk in the subdirectory in question, but only copies onto drive A those files that have been changed since the last back-up copying operation.
`backup c:*.dat a:`	This copies all files that end with DAT in the subdirectory in question onto drive A.

`backup c:\spcsword\*. dat a:`   This copies all files that end with DAT in the subdirectory named SPCSWORD onto drive A.

Note:
When you restore (recopy) the backup files, they must be restored to the same subdirectory from which they were copied.

- Press the ←┘ key.

As each disk fills up, you will be prompted to insert the next disk.

When the system prompt appears again, copying is finished.

Restore (Recopy) Files to Hard Disk (RESTORE)

RESTORE is a DOS command that is usually kept on a hard disk (otherwise, it is on the DOS disk). It is used to restore (recopy) files that have been backed up (copied) using the BACKUP command. The RESTORE command can be used for all types of files that have been backed up by means of the BACKUP command, although files that are write-protected can cause trouble.

Note:
WARNING — if you have any programs that are copy-protected (Scandinavian PC Systems programs are not copy-protected), you must not back them up using BACKUP. Moreover, you must never restore them by means of RESTORE. If you try to do so, they may become unusable.

Before you start, you must have your backup disks ready, and you must use them in numerical sequence starting with disk 1. The sequence is important.

Note:
Remember that you can only restore files to the subdirectory from which you backed them up.

- Insert the first disk in drive A.

- Type one of the following:

restore a: c:*.*

This recopies all files from drive A to the default subdirectory on the hard disk (the subdirectory that you are in).

restore a: c:*.*/s

This restores all files from drive A to the default subdirectory on the hard disk together with all the lower subdirectories (from which the files were originally copied).

restore a: c:*.*/p

Same as above, but /p causes the computer to prompt you, which means that it will ask whether each file that has been changed since you made the backup copy should be restored to the earlier form on the backup disk.

restore a: c:*.txt

This recopies all files that end with TXT from drive A to the subdirectory on the hard disk from which they were copied.

restore a: c:\spcsword*.dat

This restores all files that end in DAT from drive A to the subdirectory named SPCSWORD on the hard disk. (You must have copied them originally from SPCSWORD.)

- Press the ↵ key.

You are now asked to insert the first disk, and as soon as it is copied you are asked to insert the next, etc.

When the system prompt appears again, copying is completed.

Change Subdirectory (CD)

This command is used when you wish to change to another subdirectory.

You can change to the desired subdirectory from any other subdirectory.

- Type one of the following:

cd \	To reach the root directory.
cd \spcsword	To change to the specified subdirectory, regardless of which subdirectory you are presently in.
cd \letters\quotes	To change to the QUOTES subdirectory, which is found under LETTERS, which, in turn, is found under the root, regardless of which subdirectory you are presently in.
cd..	To change to the next higher subdirectory. In some older versions of DOS, this command requires a space before the first period. More recent versions will accept the command without the space.
cd	To see which subdirectory you are presently in.

- Press the ↵ key.

When the system prompt appears again, you will have changed to a new subdirectory. Subdirectory names must comply with the same rules as those set forth for filenames.

You can copy from and to a subdirectory using what is called a path. More information about this is presented in the DOS manual that came with your computer.

Check Disk (CHKDSK)

When you wish to check a disk or see how much memory is available on it, you can use the CHKDSK command as follows:

- Insert the DOS disk in drive A.

- Insert the disk that is to be checked in drive B.

- Type:

  `chkdsk b:`

- Press the ↵ key.

The following appears on the screen:

```
Volume USFil870210 created Feb 10, 1987 07.20a

     362496 bytes total disk space
          0 bytes in 1 hidden files
     318464 bytes in 40 user files
      44032 bytes available on disk

     655360 bytes total memory
     491136 bytes free
```

You can also use the DIR command to see how much unoccupied space is present on the disk.

Moreover, the CHKDSK command can be used to see how much memory a memory-resident program occupies, or how much memory has been installed in a computer that you're using.

- Start the computer without starting any of the memory-resident programs.

- Run CHKDSK.

- Read the last line and write this figure down.

- Start one of the memory-resident programs.

- Run CHKDSK.

- Read the last line and write this down.

The difference between what you read the first time and the second time is the amount of memory occupied by the program you started.

If you've got a hard disk, the proper command is CHKDSK C: if it's the C drive you want to inspect.

Clear Screen (CLS)

This command clears the contents of the screen.

Copy Files (COPY)

The COPY command is used to copy specific files that you designate.

- Insert the source disk containing the files that are to be copied into disk drive A.

- Insert the target disk onto which the files are to be copied into disk drive B.

- Type one of the following:

copy a:*.* b:/v
: This copies all files from disk drive A to disk drive B, and verifies the copies. Verification is called for by specifying /v; this means that after the file is copied, the computer compares the new copy with the original to be sure that they are identical. This adds time to the copying process, but it's well worth it if the file's accuracy is critical.

copy a:*.txt b:/v
: This copies all files having names with extensions of TXT from disk drive A to disk drive B and verifies the new copy.

copy a:test.txt b:/v
: This copies the file named TEXT.TXT from disk drive A to disk drive B and verifies the new copy.

`copy c:\test\*.* a:/v`	This copies all files in the TEST subdirectory on hard disk C to disk drive A and verifies the new copy.
`copy c:\test\*.* c:\temp/v`	This copies all files in the TEST subdirectory on hard disk C to the TEMP subdirectory on hard disk C and verifies the new copy.
`copy a:test.txt prn`	This copies the file named TEST.TXT to the printer. You will obtain a paper copy of the file (don't forget to make certain that the printer is ON-LINE before starting).

• Press the ⏎ key.

When the system prompt appears, copying is completed.

```
1 File(s) copied
A>
```

Change the Computer's Date (DATE)

The computer keeps a record of the date. You can change the computer's date as follows:

• Type:

date

• Press the ⏎ key.

```
Current date is Thu 01-01-1980
Enter new date (mm-dd-yy):
```

You have two choices. You may either confirm the displayed date, or enter an alternative date, i.e., the right one. Some programs depend on the computer's date being correct. This date will also be used when files are saved to record any creation or change of the disk's directory.

To confirm the displayed date, do the following:

* Press the ←┘ key.

To enter a different date, do the following:

* Type in the desired date, putting hyphens between the month and the day, and between the day and the year. For example:

  08-18-88

* Press the ←┘ key.

Delete Files (DEL)

To delete files, you can use the DEL command as follows:

* Insert the disk containing the files you wish to delete into disk drive A or B.
* Type one of the following:

  del a:*.*   This deletes all files from the disk in drive A.

  del b:*.*   This deletes all files from the disk in drive B.

  del a:*.txt   This deletes all files that end in TXT from the disk in drive A.

  del a:test.txt   This deletes the TEST.TXT file from the disk in drive A.

* Press the ←┘ key.

When the system prompt appears again on the screen, deleting is completed.

Display List of Filenames (DIR)

When you wish to display a directory containing the names, file sizes, creation dates, and creation times of all the files on a disk, you can use the DIR command as follows:

- Insert the disk in drive A.

- Type one of the following:

dir	This displays the information on all of the files on the disk in the default drive.
dir b:	This displays the information for all of the filenames for drive B.
dir *.txt	This displays all filenames that end in TXT.
dir c:\test*.txt	This displays all filenames that end in TXT in the TEST subdirectory on hard disk C.
dir /p	This displays all filenames, 23 at a time.
dir /w	This displays the filenames in five columns, but doesn't include their file sizes or creation dates and times. It's used when you want to get as many file names as possible displayed on a single screen.

- Press the ←┘ key.

Compare Disks (DISKCOMP)

You can compare the contents of two disks after you have copied them, but only if you have used DISKCOPY (see below).

- Insert the DOS disk in disk drive A.

- Type:

  ```
  diskcomp a: b:
  ```

- Press the ←┘ key.

The following will appear on the screen:

```
Insert first disk in drive A:  Insert second disk
in drive B:
Strike any key when ready
```

- Insert the first disk in disk drive A.

- Insert the disk that is to be compared with the first disk in disk drive B.

- Press the ←┘ key.

When the following appears on the screen, the comparison has shown that the contents of the disks are identical.

```
Disk compare ok
Compare more disks (Y/N)?
```

- Press the **N** key if you wish to conclude comparison. Press the **Y** key if you wish to compare other disks.

Copy Disk (DISKCOPY)

You can copy the entire content of a disk onto another disk by means of DISK-
COPY. The disk onto which you are copying need not be formatted, since this is
done automatically by DISKCOPY.

- Insert the DOS disk in disk drive A.

- Type:

  ```
  diskcopy a: b:
  ```

- Press the ←┘ key.

The following will appear on your screen:

```
Insert source disk in drive A:
Insert target disk in drive B:
Strike any key when ready
```

- Insert the disk containing what you wish to copy into disk drive A.

- Insert the disk onto which you wish to copy into disk drive B.

- Press the ←┘ key.

When the following appears on your screen, copying has been completed:

```
Copy another (Y/N)?
```

- Press the **N** key if you wish to conclude copying. Press the **Y** key if you wish to
  copy another disk.

Format Disk (FORMAT)

When you wish to prepare (format) a disk for use, proceed as follows:

- Insert the DOS disk into disk drive A.

- Type:

format b: If you wish to format a disk.

or:

format b:/s   If you wish to format a system disk
                                   that can be used to start a computer
                                   without a hard drive. While you can
                                   use a system disk to start a computer
                                   equipped with a hard drive in an
                                   emergency, you usually won't want
                                   to do this because the instructions in
                                   the AUTOEXEC.BAT or CON-
                                   FIG.SYS file, which are almost al-
                                   ways used with hard drive machines,
                                   will be unavailable.

or:

format b:/4   If you wish to format a 360 kb disk
                                   with a 1.2 Mb (high density) disk
                                   drive unit. High density disk drive
                                   units are the kinds commonly used
                                   in 286 (AT) and 386 machines.

- Press the ←⏎ key.

The following will appear on your screen:

```
Insert new disk for drive B:
and strike any key when ready
```

- Insert the disk that is to be formatted into disk drive B.

- Press the ↵ key.

When the following appears on your screen, formatting has been completed.

```
Format another (Y/N)?
```

- Press the **N** key if you wish to conclude formatting. Press the **Y** key if you wish to format another disk.

Create (Make) Subdirectory (MD)

Here you must remember that you can only create a subdirectory that is located below the one in the tree onto which you're presently logged. This means that sometimes you must first change to a subdirectory that is above the one that you are going to create.

To create a subdirectory anywhere in your directory tree, all you've got to do is first log into the root directory. Change to the root directory as follows:

- Type:

  ```
  cd \
  ```

- Press the ↵ key.

The root subdirectory is now the active subdirectory. That is to say, it is the one that will be shown when you type DIR. And when you create a new subdirectory, it will be linked to the root.

- Type:

  ```
  md test
  ```

- Press the ↵ key.

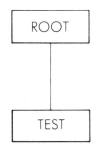

Root directory and subdirectory.

When the system prompt appears on the screen again, you will have created a subdirectory called TEST. The name of a subdirectory must comply with the same rules as those set forth for filenames. You can check to see that the subdirectory was created by issuing the DIR command.

• Type:

    dir *.

• Press the ← key.

You will see on the screen that a subdirectory called TEST has been created.

```
TEST    <DIR>    1-23-1987   12:24a
```

If you wish to change to another subdirectory, see the section headed *Change Subdirectory (CD).*

To create a subdirectory located further down the tree, just issue the same command from the root directory, but include the backslash marks and the entire path. For example:

• Type:

    md \testscore\history\europe

Press the ← key.

Change Prompt (PROMPT)

You can change the system prompt from the familiar A> or C> if so desired. If you are using a hard disk, there are many advantages to having the system prompt indicate which subdirectory you are in.

- Check that the system prompt appears on the screen.
- Type:

prompt pg

This changes the system prompt so that it presents the current subdirectory.

For example: C:\SPCSWORD>

- Press the ↵ key.

```
C:\SPCSWORD>
```

It is advisable to insert this command in your AUTOEXEC.BAT so that this type of explicit system prompt will always come up when you start your computer. There are a number of different ways to arrange the system prompt, and they are explained in the DOS manual that came with your computer.

A favorite with a lot of computer hackers is:

prompt $t pg

This changes the system prompt so that it presents both the current subdirectory and the correct time according to your computer's system clock! It's great if you're one of those persons who ends up missing appointments or a normal night's sleep due to spending too much time working on your computer. If you want to be reminded of the date instead of the time, just substitute a "d" for the "t" in this command.

To intimidate your friends who are afraid of computers, try:

prompt WHAT IS YOUR WISH MASTER? pg

By now you should be able to guess what this will do!

Remove (delete) Subdirectory (RD)

This command can be used when you wish to delete a subdirectory.

Two conditions must be fulfilled before you can delete a subdirectory, namely:

- The subdirectory must be empty, i.e., it must not contain any files or other subdirectories.

- You must be in the subdirectory on the next higher level, or in the root subdirectory.

- Type:

  `rd test`

To delete the subdirectory called TEST

- Press the ←┘ key.

You have now deleted the subdirectory.

To delete a subdirectory located further down the tree, just issue the same command from the root directory, but include the backslash marks and the entire path. For example:

- Type:

  `rd \testscore\history\europe`

- Press the ←┘ key.

Change the Computer's Time (TIME)

The computer keeps track of the current time. You can alter the time as follows:

- Type:

  `time`

- Press the ←┘ key

```
Current time is Wed 08:17:35:26
Enter correct time:
```

You have two choices, either confirm the time shown, or enter a different time.

To confirm the displayed time, do the following:

● Press the ↵ key.

To enter a new time, do the following:

● Type in the desired time, for example:

    19:18

Note that it is sufficient to give only the hour, and the minutes.

● Press the ↵ key.

The major use for TIME is to be able to display the time as part of your DOS prompt. Also, the creation time of a file is always shown in the directory display.

Type the Contents of a File (TYPE)

The type command gives you a way of looking at the contents of a file. TYPE is an internal DOS command and is readily available. The following example assumes that you have a disk in drive A, with the file TEST1.DOC on it.

● Type the following:

    type a:test1.doc

● Press the ↵ key.

The contents of the file will be displayed on your screen:

```
Hi there.
This is just one of those boring old example
texts.
Bye.
```

C. Some Common DOS Error Messages

When you're working with a computer, things do not always work out as expected the wrong disk, a forgotten colon, a wrong filename, etc. DOS has a set of error messages to tell you when you've issued an illegal command. Don't worry about the command being labeled illegal, all this means is that you've made a minor error in typing it.

This appendix lists the most common error messages, and suggests what you might have done wrong. The error messages are in alphabetical order.

Note:

The actual text of the error message may vary in some cases from that which is shown on your screen. Also, this list is by no means complete. Refer to your DOS manual for information on other messages.

Attempted write-protection violation
The disk you tried to format was write-protected. Change disks or disable the protection by removing the write-protect label from a 5.25" disk or moving the slide position from a 3.5" disk.

Bad command or file name
You have typed in a program name or command that doesn't exist in the specified, or current, directory or drive. The computer can not find what you have typed. Check your spelling.

Compare error on disk
DOS has found a difference between two disks you were comparing with the DISKCOMP command.

Data error reading drive X
The computer cannot read information from the stated disk. Try typing **R** to retry a few times. If that doesn't work, then type **A** for abort.

Duplicate filename
You tried to rename a file but have given it the same name as another existing file, or the specified file cannot be found. Check the file names on the disk, and try again.

File cannot be copied onto itself
> When trying to copy a file you gave the target file (copy) the same name as the source file. Give the copy a different name.

File not found
> The computer cannot find the file that you specified. Check that you have entered the filename correctly.

Format failure
> The disk cannot be formatted correctly. It's probably defective.

Illegal device name
> You have specified a device name that does not currently exist in your computer system. Check your typing.

Incorrect number of parameters
> You specified too many or too few options in the command.

Insufficient disk space
> The specified disk is full. Erase some files from the disk or try another one. If you get this command frequently on your hard disk, it's time to consider buying a second hard disk or upgrading to a larger one.

Insufficient memory
> There is not enough memory in your computer to perform the specified operation. This either means that you need more memory (today there's no excuse for having less than 640K) or that you're using some memory resident software that has to be unloaded before the particular program you're now trying to use can run.

Invalid date
> You specified an invalid date in response to the DATE command.

Invalid directory
> The directory you specified does not exist. Type it again, this time more carefully.

Invalid drive specification
> The drive you specified doesn't exist.

Invalid number of parameters

You specified too many or too few options in the command.

Invalid parameters

One or more of the command parameters is wrong.

Invalid path

The pathname you specified does not exist.

Invalid time

You specified an invalid time in response to the TIME command.

Nonsystem disk or disk error

You tried to start your computer with a non-system disk in drive A. Take the disk out and try again.

No paper error writing device

Your printer is out of paper, is not switched on, or is not in the PRINT READY status.

Read fault error reading drive X

The computer is unable to read data from the specified drive. This is usually a read error made by your computer. Hit **R** for retry.

If this happens again, you've somehow damaged your disk and you probably won't be able to recover the data on it unless you can get help from a friend who is very knowledgeable and has the right software. Therefore, go to your back-up disk.

What? You don't have a back-up disk? We warned you this would happen!

Note:
If this happens when you're trying to read a disk that wasn't created in your computer, the problem may be that either your disk drive or the other one is out of alignment. Try reading the disks on the machine on which it was created and/or on other machines. If it can be read on these but not on yours, have a technician check your drive's alignment.

Target disk is unusable
  The disk you tried to format is bad.

Target disk is write-protected
  The computer tried to write information on a disk that is write-protected.

Unable to create directory
  The computer cannot create the specified directory. It may already exist, or you may have specified a name with more than 8 characters or with a space in it.

Write fault error writing drive X
  The computer was unable to write data to the specified drive. This is usually a computer error. Try **R** retry. If it happens again the disk may be damaged.

Write protect error writing drive X
  The computer tried to write information on a disk that is write-protected.

D. The Keys On Your Keyboard

When confronted with a computer keyboard for the first time, novices are often frightened by the many keys other than the normal typewriter keys. The mysterious symbols and the complexity of the keyboard, do require some explanation. This appendix describes the functions of some important individual keys with which you may not be familiar.

Different keyboards

Although there are several different keyboard models, there are two main layouts. One has a group of 10 keys, marked **F1 – F10**, on the left-hand side, while the other has the same group of keys **F1 – F12** in a row at the top of the keyboard.

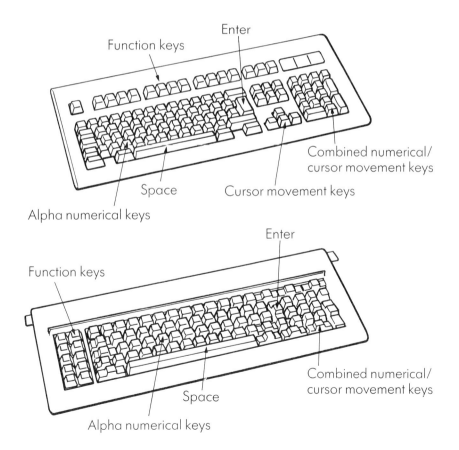

Alpha numeric keys

The keys are the normal letter and number keys, as for a standard typewriter. Upper case letters and the characters over the numbers are obtained by using the shift keys.

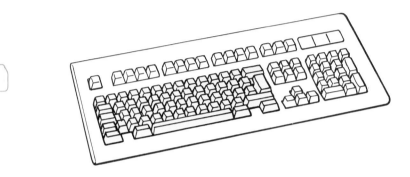

Combined numeric key pad and cursor movement keys

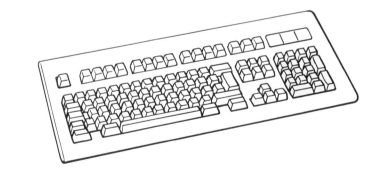

These keys can function in two ways, depending on the state of the Number Lock function. By pressing the **Num Lock** key, the Num Lock indicator will be turned on and off.

Num Lock indicator on

    With Num Lock lamp lit, these keys will work as number keys. This is useful for accounting and other number work.

Num Lock indicator off

    With Num Lock lamp not lit, these keys will work as cursor movement keys. Just how, and if, they work, will depend on the program you are running. A word processor, for example, will almost certainly use the keys to move the cursor around in a text. See also *Separate cursor movement keys*.

Separate cursor movement keys

Some keyboards will have a separate group of keys dedicated to cursor movement.

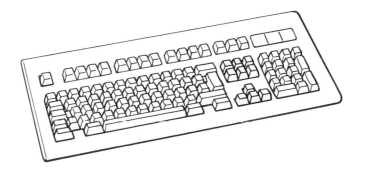

Just how, and if, they work, will depend on the program you are running.

←↑↓→   These keys are most often used to move the cursor one position in the indicated direction.

Home   This key is often used to move the cursor to the beginning of a line, screen display, or text.

End   This key is often used to move the cursor to the end of a line, screen display, or text.

Page Up   This key is often used to move the cursor to the beginning of a screen display, or text.

Page Down   This key is often used to move the cursor to the end of screen display, or text.

Insert   This key is often used to control how new text is inserted into a text. Pressing the key will often toggle between an insert and overwrite mode. Insert means that text will be inserted at the cursor's position and the following text moved over. The overwrite mode will cause text entered at the cursor's position to replace that which already exists.

Delete   This key is often used to delete the character at the cursor's position.

Function keys

The function keys are grouped on the left-hand side of the keyboard (**F1** – **F10**), or in a row at the top of it (**F1** – **F12**).

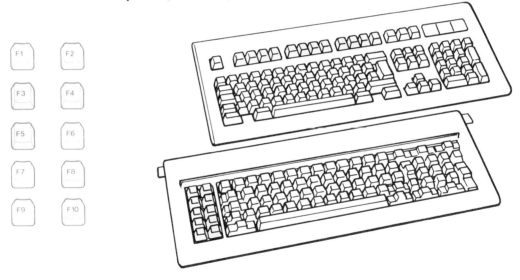

These keys are used by application programs, and will be assigned different functions for each program, and sometimes different functions at different points within the same program. Think of these as "shortcut" keys, since they're usually used to let one keystroke do the job of many.

For example, **F1** could be defined to save a text in a word processor program, to show a help text in a communications program, or to delete an entry in a database program. In each case, without the use of the function key, you might have to issue several different commands to make the program do what you want.

Special keys

The remainder of this appendix is dedicated to other keys, which have their own special importance.

Enter key

The **Enter** key is perhaps the most important key of all. It is mainly used in two ways.

When typing in commands, instructions, and data, you usually have to press this key to confirm your input. In such cases, although you may have typed in a command, it is not followed until you have pressed the Enter key.

A word processor program will require you to press the Enter key to mark the end of a paragraph, and move the cursor down to the next line. This is similar to the CR (Carriage Return) key of a standard typewriter.

Backspace key

The **Backspace** is normally used to delete the character immediately to the left of the cursor.

Caps Lock key

This key is used to lock the alphabetical keys, **A – Z**, in their upper cases, as for a standard typewriter.

Ctrl key

The **Ctrl** key (short for Control) is used together with other keys, to perform special operations in an applications program.

Alt key

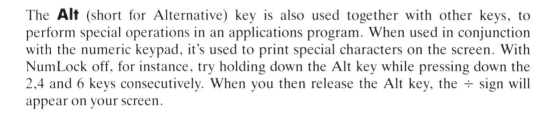

The **Alt** (short for Alternative) key is also used together with other keys, to perform special operations in an applications program. When used in conjunction with the numeric keypad, it's used to print special characters on the screen. With NumLock off, for instance, try holding down the Alt key while pressing down the 2,4 and 6 keys consecutively. When you then release the Alt key, the ÷ sign will appear on your screen.

Esc key

The **Esc** key (short for Escape) is usually used in applications programs to exit a part of that program or to undo a change you have made.

Tab key

This key is normally used to jump between predefined margin positions, or between input fields.

Print Screen key

This key will result in a copy of the monitor display being sent to the printer for printing. Many keyboards require you to press the ⇧ and **PrtSc** keys together.

Note that some programs may disable this function and not permit it to be used.

More About Your Keyboard

The keyboard has its own small buffer, or memory, to store up to 11 key strokes. These will be held until the computer is ready to print them on the screen. If this buffer gets filled, which usually happens when the computer is doing a lot of processing and doesn't have time to check for keyboard inputs as frequently as it normally does, the computer will beep. This tells you that no more information can currently be received from the keyboard. If you're a very fast typist and you're using a program that slows up keyboard input (communications programs are famous for this), there are several programs that can increase the buffer's size so that you won't have to wait for your computer to catch up to you.

It is also possible that keys will have an auto-repeat function. This means that if you keep a key depressed, the computer will see this as if you are repeatedly pressing that key.

E. Producing Graphics Characters with the Alt Key

Your computer is not only capable of producing letters and numbers, it can also produce many graphic characters. These characters can be used with certain programs, for example, to create boxes and lines.

To write these characters, which are not displayed on any of the keys on your keyboard, you need to press the **Alt** key, in conjunction with a number code, using the number keys on the right-hand side of the keyboard.

A table of available characters is displayed below. To obtain a character in the table, you must look up its number code. The example below will type an Ä character.

- Hold down the **Alt** key.
- Type in the code number for the desired character, using the number key pad on the right-hand side of the keyboard, for example:

  142

- Release the **Alt** key.

This will not necessarily work for all programs or printers, since some use their own character sets. In such cases, you should consult the appropriate manual.

Character table

21	= §	69	= E	107	= k	145	= æ	183	= ⊓	221	= ▌
32	=	70	= F	108	= l	146	= Æ	184	= ┐	222	= ▐
33	= !	71	= G	109	= m	147	= ô	185	= ╣	223	= ▀
34	= "	72	= H	110	= n	148	= ö	186	= ║	224	= α
35	= #	73	= I	111	= o	149	= ò	187	= ╗	225	= β
36	= $	74	= J	112	= p	150	= û	188	= ╝	226	= Γ
37	= %	75	= K	113	= q	151	= ù	189	= ╜	227	= π
38	= &	76	= L	114	= r	152	= ÿ	190	= ╛	228	= Σ
39	= ´	77	= M	115	= s	153	= Ö	191	= ┐	229	= σ
40	= (	78	= N	116	= t	154	= Ü	192	= └	230	= μ
41	=)	79	= O	117	= u	155	= ¢	193	= ┴	231	= τ
42	= *	80	= P	118	= v	156	= £	194	= ┬	232	= Φ
43	= +	81	= Q	119	= w	157	= ¥	195	= ├	233	= θ
44	= ,	82	= R	120	= x	158	= R	196	= ─	234	= Ω
45	= −	83	= S	121	= y	159	= ƒ	197	= ┼	235	= δ
46	= .	84	= T	122	= z	160	= á	198	= ╞	236	= ∞
47	= /	85	= U	123	= {	161	= í	199	= ╟	237	= ø
48	= 0	86	= V	124	= ¦	162	= ó	200	= ╚	238	= ∈
49	= 1	87	= W	125	= }	163	= ú	201	= ╔	239	= ∩
50	= 2	88	= X	126	= ~	164	= ñ	202	= ╩	240	= ≡
51	= 3	89	= Y	127	= ⌂	165	= Ñ	203	= ╦	241	= ±
52	= 4	90	= Z	128	= Ç	166	= ª	204	= ╠	242	= ≥
53	= 5	91	= [	129	= ü	167	= º	205	= ═	243	= ≤
54	= 6	92	= \	130	= é	168	= ¿	206	= ╬	244	= ⌠
55	= 7	93	=]	131	= â	169	= ⌐	207	= ╧	245	= ⌡
56	= 8	94	= ^	132	= ä	170	= ¬	208	= ╨	246	= ÷
57	= 9	95	= _	133	= à	171	= ½	209	= ╤	247	= ≈
58	= :	96	= `	134	= å	172	= ¼	210	= ╥	248	= °
59	= ;	97	= a	135	= ç	173	= ¡	211	= ╙	249	= ·
60	= <	98	= b	136	= ê	174	= «	212	= ╘	250	= ·
61	= =	99	= c	137	= ë	175	= »	213	= ╒	251	= √
62	= >	100	= d	138	= è	176	= ░	214	= ╓	252	= ⁿ
63	= ?	101	= e	139	= ï	177	= ▒	215	= ╫	253	= ²
64	= @	102	= f	140	= î	178	= ▓	216	= ╪	254	= ■
65	= A	103	= g	141	= ì	179	= │	217	= ┘	255	=
66	= B	104	= h	142	= Ä	180	= ┤	218	= ┌		
67	= C	105	= i	143	= Å	181	= ╡	219	= █		
68	= D	106	= j	144	= É	182	= ╢	220	= ▄		

F. Creating a MASTER Diskette

This book is sold in two different versions, a "book only" edition and a "book/diskette" combination. The diskette that comes with the latter is called the MASTER diskette. Most of its files extend the breadth of the book, but aren't referenced in the text. However, there are a few brief text files that are needed to do some of the activities.

If you don't have the diskette, please create the following files on a disk you should label MASTER. You can create these files using any word processing program in less than 10 minutes. Save these files in ASCII format (some word processors call these TEXT files). If you don't know how to do this, or don't have a word processor, ask someone else to create them for you.

File name: EXAMPLE.TXT
Hi there,
As you may have guessed by the name, this is an example text file.
Bye.

File name: TEST1.DOC
Hi there,
This is just one of those boring old example texts.
Bye.

File name: TEST2.DOC
Hi there,
You guessed it, another boring old example text.
Bye.

File name: ANOTHER.TXT
Hi there,
You guessed it, another boring old example text.
Bye.

If you have trouble creating these files, you can call *1-800-288-7226* to order a MASTER diskette for $9.95 plus $4.95 for shipping & handling. This includes the needed text files plus a private mastery test, a 150-lesson typing tutor, a communications simulator, and a great DOS utility.

Index

Program License Agreement

Scandinavian PC Systems produces high-quality computer programs and sells them at very low prices. Our business idea is to market programs and manuals in volumes high enough to justify our low price.

We thus respectfully request that you observe the following:

1. **You may:**

    a. Use this program on a single computer.

    b. Make copies of this program for your own use.

    c. Transfer this program to a third party who accepts these conditions. If you transfer the program, you must transfer all copies to the same third party. Any that are not transferred must be destroyed.

2. **You must not:**

    a. Use this program on more than one computer. By way of example, an instructor must purchase a separate program for each computer used by his students or trainees.

    b. Disassemble or decompile the program.

    c. Export the program without the written permission of *Scandinavian PC Systems*

Warranty

Scandinavian PC Systems herewith warrants that on delivery your diskette is free of material faults and processing errors. Beyond this, *Scandinavian PC Systems* does not provide any type of warranty regarding the program's characteristics and does not warrant that it will be suitable for your applications. Neither does *Scandinavian PC Systems* assume any responsibility whatsoever for any damages that may occur in connection with the use of the program.